TROPHY ENVY

(As Heard on the Public Radio Show "Weekend Radio")

Mark Levy

TROPHY ENVY

(As Heard on the Public Radio Show "Weekend Radio")

Mark Levy

Cover and Interior Art by
John Ed Bon Fed

Belanger Books
2018

Trophy Envy (As Heard on the Public Radio Show "Weekend Radio")
© 2018 by Mark Levy
Cover and Interior Artwork © 2018 John Ed Bon Fed
Print and Digital Editions© 2018 Belanger Books, LLC
ISBN-13: 978-1717235756
ISBN-10: 1717235751

For information contact Belanger Books, LLC
61 Theresa Ct.
Manchester, NH 03103
derrick@belangerbooks.com
www.belangerbooks.com

Edited by Derrick Belanger
Book and Cover design by Brian Belanger

Essays taken from the author's *Weekend Radio* performances, Robert Conrad, host, broadcast weekly on Public Radio

To Arlene

I can never disappoint
the person who loves and
believes in me so much.

Table of Contents

III. COMING AND GOING

IV. YOU CALL THIS WORK?

Foreword

First, some arcane broadcasting history. Back in 1954, a junior in the Speech School at Northwestern University secured an announcer's job at the now legendary Chicago classical music station WFMT. He was the replacement for Mike Nichols. (Yes, that Mike Nichols — satirical comedian and stage and screen director). Nichols had created a unique Saturday night program of folk music, Broadway and especially comedy. It was called *The Midnight Special*. Although the new announcer never got to host *The Midnight Special*, he continued to work at WFMT (excerpt for a two year hiatus for a U.S. Army all-expense paid vacation in Hawaii). Then in 1960, he became the program director of a new classical FM station in Detroit — WDTM. There, inspired by *The Midnight Special*, he created a program called *WDTM Saturday Night*, an unabashed copy of the WFMT program. This lasted until 1962, when he and a new found partner purchased a fledgling FM station in Cleveland with the call letters of WDGO. After it was announced that he and his partner were buying the station, the entire staff left. So in the interim while the FCC was gazing at its navel on deciding whether to approve the deal, the NU graduate and his partner offered to run the station until the FCC transferred the license.

With *WDTM Saturday Night* having been a success, *WDGO Saturday Night* was established, and when the license was transferred on November 1, 1962, the call letters were changed to WCLV and the two hour mélange of folk music, Broadway, esoterica, and especially comedy, became *WCLV Saturday Night*.

i

Now, fast forward to 1982. *WCLV Saturday Night* had become such a Cleveland success, that it was decided that a national spinoff should be established, and the one hour show would be called *Weekend Radio*. It, too, would be a success, garnering some 100 plus stations from Guam to Alaska to Florida, with the stations paying money to carry the show, something that doesn't happen much anymore.

Eventually, the wife of our hero persuaded him that there were other things to do on Saturday night besides go to a radio studio and present a three hour air show. This made sense to him, because *Weekend Radio* was a distillation of the three hour show, and why should he continue doing two separate programs a week? So in 1989, the run of WCLVSN came to an end, replaced on WCLV by *Weekend Radio*, heard Saturdays at 10:00 PM.

We fast forward again to the late 20th Century, when short humorous essays by a Cleveland writer, Jan C. Snow, were added. Then the program manager of WXXI-FM in Rochester, John Profitt, who was doing a somewhat similar miscellaneous show called *Salmagundi*, suggested that *Weekend Radio* might be interested in commentary from a wild Britisher by the name of Richard Holland-Bolton, who lives in Plano, Texas. So he of the hyphenated name was added to the weekly mix, alternating with Ms. Snow.

Once again, we fast forward, this time to 2007, when our broadcaster received a letter and selection of essays from a patent attorney in Binghamton, New York, where the local public station, WSKG, carries *Weekend Radio*. The subjects were varied, wry personal histories, comment on social conventions, musings. These were not belly laugh causing, but resulting in smiles and nods of recognition. His name is Mark Levy, and he was told that *Weekend Radio* was interested, but the features needed to be shorter — about three to four minutes — and his pay would be local and national recognition and glory, and maybe a Tortuga Rum Cake at holiday time. So, now in the year of our Lord 2018, The Wisdom of Mark Levy continues on *Weekend Radio*, rotating with the two other radio essayists. Mark has moved his base of operations from Binghamton to Boynton Beach, Florida, and now to Evergreen, Colorado where it is often warmer in the winter than Binghamton. There, he, on occasion, retires to a deep, dark, damp writers cave and creates a half year or so of features at one sitting, essays with such varied titles as "Building Insult Vocabularies," "My First Puppy," and "Back to Basics — Roman Numerals." He then records the material for shipping off to WCLV. He has a daughter in Cleveland, whom he visits periodically, and visits WCLV. But since he lived in Florida until a few years ago, and The Cleveland Orchestra has four residencies there each winter, and the Saturday night concerts are broadcast back to Cleveland, he and his significant other drive down to Miami to attend the concerts and have dinner with the concert commentator, who is also the host of *Weekend Radio*. And Mark does receive a Tortuga Rum Cake, or sometimes a Racine Kringle, at holiday time as thanks for another year of witty and wry commentaries that don't necessarily cause belly laughs, but smiles and perhaps, nods of recognition.

Robert Conrad
President
WCLV
Cleveland Orchestra Broadcast Service
Host: *Weekend Radio*

Preface

By day I am a patent attorney who happens to have a graduate degree in creative writing. As a patent attorney, I am a midwife for inventors. I don't usually invent anything (I like to use the word "conceive," consistent with my metaphor), but I help my clients obtain patents so they can make money from their ideas.

When I'm not working on a patent application (and sometimes when I am), I sometimes ask myself questions. They're typically short questions, like "why are we still working 40 hours per week?" and "why do old people move slower than young people, when they have less time left to move at all?" and "why do all states have two-letter postal abbreviations, even if no other state starts with the same letter?"

I used to go to bed thinking about these things, hoping to remember the questions the next morning so I could look up the answers in my local library. But now with the Internet, I don't have to wait until the next morning and I don't have to find the answers in obscure books. I can get them almost immediately at my computer or my cell phone. I can access just about all the information in the world by touching or even talking into my phone. Pretty cool.

It occurred to me that if I wanted answers to these types of admittedly silly questions, maybe other people did, too. Then I found a quirky radio show called *Weekend Radio* on the Public Radio network. It had a sprinkling of classical music, comedy albums — many being British — and audio essays.

"Hey," thought I, "I wonder if there's a place on that show for me to share my questions and observations."

So I recorded a couple of my essays on CDs and mailed them to the producer of that show in Cleveland, Ohio: Robert Conrad. He thought they were interesting or foolish enough to broadcast, and the rest is history. I also funneled some of my essays in written form to the *Mensa Bulletin* and to an impressive but little-known online magazine called *ragazine.cc*.

What I hadn't bargained for was a constant need for more material. Fortunately, I shared the weekly broadcast with two other essayists, so the pieces I recorded myself aired only tri-weekly. As it turned out, that wasn't a problem for me, since I think of many, many new questions within those three weeks. The Internet helps me research answers and sometimes moves me in unexpected directions.

Since the essays in this book were written for audio taping and radio broadcast on *Weekend Radio*, you may see certain references to the show or to Robert Conrad. You may even see some pronunciation hints for the narrator (me). Feel free to ignore them or, better yet, imagine you're listening to me read them.

Mark Levy
Evergreen, Colorado

I

IT WASN'T FUNNY AT THE TIME

Trophy Envy

My archery trophy sits atop the mantel of my fireplace. It's almost as high as the living room ceiling. It's the biggest trophy I've ever seen, about four feet high. The base is a solid rectangle of marble, four inches by six inches and about half an inch high. Anchored to the base, rise up two majestic Greek columns, also of marble, and some sort of imitation gold insignia spanning the two uprights. Then there's another tier above the columns with another large, marble platform and a column above that. It must be 14 pounds, the weight of an average Thanksgiving turkey.

The statue itself is gold-colored plastic and depicts a slender male archer with perfect form and with his bow extended. There's a black metal plate attached to the front edge of the base and it says, "Mark Levy, First Prize, International Archery Competition."

The whole trophy is impressive as heck.

In fact, it often elicits admiring comments from guests who visit my house, which was the whole point in displaying it in my living room in the first place.

I have to admit that I'm more than a little proud of the trophy. It really dominates the room, especially from the point of view of a guest whom I direct to the cushy chair that faces it.

The conversation usually goes something like this:

"Wow, what a trophy," they say.

I just smile, modestly.

"Is that yours?"

"Yup," I admit.

"I didn't know you were into archery."

1

I continue to smile. Sometimes I say something like, "Well, I don't like to brag."

"When did you get that?"

"A few years ago," I say. "I'm a little embarrassed that it's so big. Barely fits above the fireplace."

I can keep the conversation going for a while, but at some point, I usually have had enough basking in their respect. So I confess that, although it's my trophy — I mean, I own it — I didn't really win it. I merely purchased it at a garage sale for fifty cents.

Oh, and the name plate cost an additional two bucks a few years ago. Turns out, and lucky for me, trophy suppliers don't really question authenticity of the name plates they produce. If you want them to engrave something, they will. Truth to tell, I could see that my local trophy maker was pretty impressed with the size of my trophy, too.

Dead silence usually ensues after my confession.

"I'm looking for a fishing trophy to make it a set," I say. "Do you think that would be too much? Would people actually believe I won... I mean I own... both of them?"

Confessions of a Book Collector

When I was nine years old, I made a mistake I'm still paying for. The mistake resulted in having to add a 1,500 square foot addition to a house I used to own. Recently, my darling, long-suffering wife and I had to purchase a condo that's easily four times too big for just the two of us.

I could have decided to collect postage stamps or even jewelry, back when I was nine. Collections like those wouldn't have needed much space. But in 1958 I decided to buy a 35¢ paperback collection of science fiction short stories entitled, *Men, Martians and Machines* by Eric Frank Russell. (By the way, you can purchase the softcover book today online for three or four bucks or from a book dealer in Canada for $107.) I suppose I could have borrowed the book from my local library, but the cover was so attractive, I knew I had to own the book. Although 35¢ was not easy to come by for a pre-adolescent on a 25¢ weekly allowance, I thought the investment would be worthwhile.

Fast forward 56 years. I now have 11,278 books and a condo with six — count 'em, six! — bathrooms. My wife and I don't need three bathrooms apiece, but it's impossible to find a condo with one bedroom and a library big enough to hold 33 bookcases.

So you see the magnitude of the mistake I made over half a century ago. My library has grown to include some thousand Sherlockian volumes, ten dozen annotated books, complete collections of *the Best American Short Stories* going back to 1915, *O. Henry Award Prize Stories*, books on inventors and their

3

inventions, books on movie making, books on writing, and 700 books of limericks.

In my collection I even have books on book collecting and the weirdoes who collect them. I especially enjoy books that refer to the "gentle madness" and the stories of obsessed people who bought multiple houses for their books or packed their house so tightly with books, there was no place to stand or lie down. When I read those stories, I can say, "I'm not *that* bad... yet."

Now that I have many complete sets of science fiction anthologies and collections of books by certain authors who specialize in mystery and popular fiction, I've entered into a new phase of book collecting. I'm on a quest to meet as many authors as I can and ask them to sign my copies of their books. I'm specializing in octogenarian authors, since I enjoy accomplishing tasks under time pressure.

In the last few years, I was able to meet the mystery short story writer, Ed Hoch, before he passed away. He was gracious enough to spend a couple of hours with me autographing a good portion of the 850 short stories he had published in the last four decades. I traveled to Rochester to meet him and his lovely wife.

Charles Harness was another find. He passed away about a decade ago at the age of 90, but not until he had signed 25 of his books for me in Maryland. Charles — he told me I could call him Charles — was an accomplished author in the '40s and '50s, but then decided to become a patent attorney and pursue that career for 40 years. And then he came back to writing science fiction. How's that for a life story? One of his later stories concerned a legal case in the future, when patent infringement became a crime punishable by death. I ask you, how can you not like an author who takes intellectual property violations so seriously?

J.P. Donleavy is turning out to be more elusive than I would have thought. He has what he calls a cottage but most of us would call a mansion, if not a castle, situated on 180 acres of land in Ireland. He doesn't answer my letters and, if this goes on, I'm afraid I'll have to pay him a personal visit. I don't know exactly where he lives, but how difficult can it be to find him? Ireland's a small country.

And speaking of reclusive authors, I once traveled 10 hours by car with a trunkful of books to meet up with a prolific author who values his privacy and requested that I not mention his name, not take his photo, not disclose his phone number, and not reveal the year of his birth. We spent a truly wonderful and memorable two hours discussing and signing 80 books. I can't tell you where he lives. In fact, I've probably said too much already.

I travel to book fairs and conventions around the country. This task I've set for myself is a breeze now that I live within a few miles of the south Florida independent book store, *Books and Books*. There, every week authors are invited to read some of their works and sign books.

But if the authors are mobile enough to visit a bookstore for a signing, they are nowhere near old enough for me.

Fan Mail

I get a heck of a lot of fan mail nowadays. Maybe not as much as Paris Hilton or that famous soccer guy, but for me, the number of letters I receive is overwhelming. Some of the messages come in the form of emails and occasional faxes, but much of it still arrives by the people who we used to call mailmen.

I thought I'd share one recent letter with you, which is typical of the sort of mail I receive.

"Dear Mr. Levy," it begins.

"Your essays are superb. I look forward to your piece every time I tune in to *Weekend Radio*. Unfortunately, as you know, you're not on the air every week. When your time slot is appropriated by another regular essayist, I have to deal with severe depression for many days. I am not a young woman anymore, so coping with depression/anxiety can be debilitating. I am often on the verge of suicide, in fact.

"But enough about me. What I like about your essays are your observations about society. They always strike a chord in me. Whether you're speaking about technology or human nature or national holidays, you get to the heart of the matter in an enjoyable and erudite way. I'm enthralled by your metaphors, enraptured by your cadence, and enthused by your *joire de vivre*. Your presentation is pitch perfect, as far as I'm concerned. I've advised all of my friends and all of the relatives I still talk to, to catch your witticisms on the weekend.

"You are articulate, honest, and passionate — qualities that I've heard only in reenactments of Abraham Lincoln's addresses. Sometimes, in my wilder fantasies, I think you might jump clear out of my radio and into my living room, bigger than life, pontificating and gesticulating, like some over-energetic evangelical preacher running for political office.

"I also love the way you wrap up your essays. They drone on just the right length and then peter out with a thought-provoking conclusion that has me smiling for the rest of the day.

"All in all, Mr. Levy, I believe you are actually the best thing to happen to radio since that Macaroni guy invented it.

"Your admiring fan, etc., etc."

As I say, that's typical of the sort of mail I receive and of course I'm very appreciative. So keep those laudatory letters coming, Mom. I love you, too.

Listen to This

A little while ago, I was shocked to hear my first essay broadcast on *Weekend Radio*. Shocked, not because of the subject matter. After all, you wouldn't believe how much time I spend working on these little gems, to the neglect of my livelihood, my family and even my health. At least, that's the excuse I give my doctor when I stray from his diet.

No, I wasn't shocked at the subject matter, but at the delivery of my essay. My voice sounded, well, whiny. It was not at all as smooth and relaxed as, oh, say, Robert Conrad's. It sounded more like a nervous Minnie Mouse, to tell the truth. If I want to sound suave and urbane, that will take an awful lot of effort. Stay tuned.

But the tinny sound of my voice got me thinking that it might not be all my fault. After all, I was listening in my kitchen to the little radio that teeters precariously beneath one of my kitchen cabinets, with its fragile antenna dangling like an anorexic worm. That radio has a single speaker less than 2" in diameter. With a speaker like that, let's face it, even Sir Laurence Olivier would come out sounding like a chipmunk.

I like to believe that all of you listeners have state-of-the-art audio systems that make me sound at least half as sophisticated as I think I am. Oh, and about 15 pounds lighter, but that's another subject.

As it happened, that night I went to a concert of the Binghamton Philharmonic. I settled into my seat a few minutes before the concert started. It occurred to me, as I looked around at the gray-haired men and women in the audience, that a very high percentage of them had hearing aids. This is to be expected in an older crowd, and there are few crowds as old, nowadays, as concert-goers.

So here I was, amidst a thousand or so octogenarians, preparing to hear Mozart. And that's when a sense of pity overcame me. I realized that most of the audience was about to hear Mozart's famous Symphony No. 40 in g minor through the equivalent of a telephone... and a cell phone at that. Some 65 classically trained musicians, playing every orchestra instrument from piccolos to double basses, had rehearsed for hours, and had forsaken their friends and family on a Saturday night to perform in dark gowns and tuxedos for a fidgety group of hearing-impaired codgers.

Suddenly, I didn't feel so bad any more about my little pieces being broadcast to portable transistor radios in noisy kitchens. At least I don't have to wear a tuxedo.

A Mouse in the Bed

An exquisite delay occurs, when I'm in repose, between the faint, almost ephemeral sensation of a critter's whiskers at my ankles and my moment of realization that I am being visited, in bed, by a mouse. The delay is only a fraction of a second, but it's enough to shoot adrenalin into my bloodstream like fuel injected into a carburetor. And not unlike the gasoline that soon explodes in an engine, my heart immediately begins to pound at three times its normal rate.

It's not my heartbeat, however, that I notice at first. That sensation of blood coursing through my veins and arteries at flow rates for which they were never designed dawns on me only seconds later, after I breathe — in deep heaves — while shaking like a leaf in a hurricane. No, what I am aware of after that slight, yet interminable delay between the mouse's whisker touch and recognition, is weightlessness.

I am assailed both with the nervous shock to my system — no less traumatic than feeling a .45 caliber bullet penetrate my rib cage — and with incredulity that my body is capable of perfect, complete, vertical levitation from a horizontal position. In fact, it matters not whether I was lying on my side, back or even stomach when the initial contact was made. My body rises a full six inches, spontaneously and effortlessly, lifting my sheet and blanket with me, completely off my mattress.

A surprising and pleasant benefit of increased blood circulation, of course, is my heightened cognition. My brain, in other words, has a lucid moment. I quickly realize that the remainder of the evening should be spent in someone else's bed. So I leave my former abode to my newfound, little gray friend.

Movies I Regret

I make amateur movies and I've been doing that for years. They are somewhere between home movies and Hollywood productions. Okay, perhaps they're a bit closer to home movies, because they feature the friends and those members of my family who can be coerced into amateur acting in front of my camcorder.

I suspect that many movie makers have regrets about some of their work. I'm one of them. I'm not talking merely about not winning an Academy Award® this year (or last year or the year before, now that I think of it). And I'm not talking about failing to entice Kim Basinger or George Clooney to act for free in one of my amateur productions. I'm referring to the movies themselves that I should have created differently.

The worst thing about knowing what I should have done is that I have to watch my movie over and over again when friends come to visit or I am invited to someone else's home. (Being invited to others' homes is occurring less frequently, too, but I like to think it's not all my fault. Anyway, that's a subject for another essay.) The audience may not notice anything amiss, but every time I see one of my defective movies, the mistakes are more evident than they were the last time.

Not only do I know what doesn't work so well; I usually also know how I could have made the movie perfect. Hindsight is 20/20, as my grandfather used to say. Ironically, he became legally blind in his final years, so his aphorisms don't always ring true. He also said that if you have a good suit, you'll never go hungry in a big city. But I digress.

Often, as occurs in other art forms, the solution to perfecting a movie is trivial. Just like adding a teaspoon of baking powder to a cake recipe might make all the difference, a half-second cutaway close-up or a reaction shot inserted into a video sequence might be all that's missing for the sequence to gel.

Before finalizing the movie, I sometimes ask another person to review my work. That can be very helpful. Of course, I wouldn't dream of paying him or her for that service. Wouldn't want to jeopardize my hard-fought amateur movie making standing, you know.

Sometimes I don't notice the error in my movie until months after I've completed it. It wouldn't take me much time to revise the movie, assuming I have the appropriate shots in my out-takes. But I resist going back and revising instead of moving forward to the next project. Now that I know what I did wrong, I say to myself, I don't have time to revise it, but I'll be sure not to make the same mistake the next time.

There's a perverse comfort in knowing that, every time I embark on another movie adventure, I'll be able to go on to make fresh, new mistakes.

My Life's Disappointments

Unless you're a rock star or the President, your life hasn't turned out exactly as you had hoped. Maybe you have a good job, you live in a nice house and your brother-in-law doesn't engage in food fights at family gatherings. But let's face it: you could have a nicer car, you could be taking more vacations to exotic locations, and you could be dining on steaks and lobster tails more often in a perfect world.

I'm a bit disappointed myself, I have to admit. But it's not the material things I covet. I mean how many homes do I really need? How fast does my car have to go? And how many pounds of caviar do I have to consume before I'm sick of the stuff?

No, I'm disappointed in a few things that never occurred for me or for anyone, no matter how rich or influential. For example, growing up in the 50s and 60s and reading a lot of science fiction, I came to look forward to — even expect — certain technical developments that haven't occurred yet.

Why aren't we vacationing on the moon colonies by now? It's been more than 40 years since we landed people on the moon. Forty years from the Wright Brothers' flight, we had routine trans-continental and trans-oceanic passenger flights; forty years after Thomas Edison's phonograph invention, or Henry Ford's Model A automobile or Alexander Graham Bell's telephone, a great percentage of Americans had phonographs, cars, and telephones. But space travel after 40 years? Not so much.

Chances of seeing even the first manned exploration of Mars — much less flights for tourists — in my lifetime? About zero percent. Now that's disappointing.

Another frustration for me and possibly a good number of you is the fact that we won't be able to live forever. We can cure many, but not all diseases, we can repair or replace organs and limbs, but no matter what, we all die.

It's sobering to realize that we are the only generation to know that immortality is around the corner, but we probably won't live to see it. In the year 1750, no one expected to live forever; and 500 years from now, there should be no medical obstacles. Old age will be cured. But we are now the first to know where we're heading and to know we, individually, won't get there before time runs out for each of us. Now that's disappointing.

Finally, I really would have liked to do a bit of time traveling. Wouldn't it be nice to see history being made? Just name the event and get a front row seat. But I'm even more curious to see the future. What will society be like? How about technology? Oh, the things we will be able to accomplish are sure to be awesome. Alas, the only way for me to get to the future is by moving in the slow lane, along with the rest of you, day by day, one minute per minute.

Okay, the time travel desire is far-fetched, I know, but what about space travel and immortality? The fact is, no one — no matter how rich, powerful, or important — can achieve those goals now. And somehow, knowing that not only I, but no one can get there in our lifetimes is the most disappointing thing of all.

My Short Life as a Potential Criminal

When I was 16, I discovered a book at the Union Turnpike public library and fell in love with it. In fact, I had an overwhelming desire to own it. So here was my plan. I was going to confess to losing the book, so I could pay for it and keep it. See, I couldn't locate a hard cover edition at my local bookstore and this seemed like the most logical way to obtain it. My approach was basically foolproof.

The middle-aged woman behind the desk had a round head covered with white hair. A pair of white-rimmed reading glasses hung from a beaded eyeglass chain. She sensed my presence and looked up. "Can I help you?" Her voice was old but strong.

"I lost a book," I said. "Where do I pay for it?"

She cocked her head, as if she couldn't believe what she was hearing. Her eyes were steady, insightful, sizing me up.

"Oh my," she said.

It struck me as odd that people still said "oh my" in this age of slang, rap, and MTV. Even Grandma Anna didn't speak like that.

"Well, I guess I'll have to pay for it," I said, trying to sound resigned.

"What is your name, young man?"

"I'm Mark Levy."

"And the title of the volume?"

"The volume is... was... the volume... the book was DEATH IN THE AFTERNOON."

"Ernest Hemingway," she declared, nodding but still locking her eyes onto mine. "Some say it's one of Hemingway's

15

best books. A bit too gruesome for my taste, I'm afraid. But many consider it the best book about bullfighting."

"Yes." I smiled nervously. "I was really enjoying it. I checked it out three weeks ago. Now it's due and it's gone."

"Did you look for it in your room?"

"Yes, I did. I looked everywhere. It's just lost."

"But did you search under your bed? You'd be surprised how many people misplace library books under their bed."

I hesitated. I could hardly lie to the kindly woman with the piercing eyes. "No," I admitted, "I didn't look under my bed."

She brightened. "Okay, then. You go home and look under your bed and if you find the book, we won't charge you for the additional day rental."

The conclusion seemed so logical, so final, I could do nothing but turn slowly and slouch out of the library, my head down, my feet shuffling. This wasn't going the way I had expected. But tomorrow, I knew, nothing would stop me. I would own the book, free and clear.

The next day after school, I was back at the library. The same kindly clerk sat behind the desk. She recognized me.

"How did it go, Mr. Levy? Any luck under your bed?"

"No, ma'am," I replied. I had never used "ma'am" in my life, but somehow this library clerk elicited that sort of response. She seemed to be a cross between Torquemada, the Spanish inquisitor, and a nun.

"I didn't find it under the bed. I'm afraid it's lost. I'm happy to pay for it, though. Can you tell me how much it will cost?"

The library clerk shook her head and made a tsk tsk sound barely opening her mouth. Although I had often seen it in print, I had never actually heard tsk tsk vocalized.

She ignored my request for a price.

16

"Let's think about where you were the last time you had the book. Were you on a bus, perhaps? Or maybe" — she glanced knowingly at my sneakers — "at a basketball game?"

"No, I'm pretty sure I was home the last time I saw it."

"Well, what about your parents' car? Could you have left it there?"

I hesitated again, tightening my lips. I met her eyes and couldn't continue the charade. Despondently I replied, "I suppose I could have."

"Well, then, I suggest you search the car. Sometimes books slide between seats or under them, you know."

So once again, I turned towards the exit and shuffled my way out of her presence.

The third day, I was back empty-handed again. I merely shook my head at the shrewd library clerk's inquisitive glance. I nervously fingered the five dollar bill in the left pocket of my jeans.

"You are in quite a quandary, Mr. Levy," she said, sympathy oozing from her old, watery blue eyes. I was forced to agree with her. Quandary was the exact word I was searching for. I just wanted to pay for the stupid book. I had the money, but she was thwarting me from carrying out my simple plan. It was like playing chess against a grand master.

"How about your school locker? Have you checked that?"

"No," I admitted. I hoped that my tone of voice would be interpreted more as embarrassment that I hadn't thought of that than as frustration at my inability to execute my scheme. I hadn't checked my school locker or checked my parents' car or checked under my bed, because I knew damn well where the book was. It was calmly resting on a shelf in my room. But I was simply no good at this prevarication. I was defeated and I knew it. This game could continue for the rest of my life, or until the library

17

clerk retired from her job. I was disinclined to think that the latter event would occur first. So I left once again, feeling even more dejected than I had in the last three days.

On the fourth day, I returned with the book under my arm. The library clerk smiled as if I were triumphantly strutting around a bullfighting arena. She pointed to me, silently, her hand shaking slightly, beaming like the fiancé of a winning Hemingway matador.

I smiled back, ruefully, in spite of myself. I handed the book over the desktop to her. "I just knew you would find it, Mr. Levy," she declared, riffling through the pages and to the back cover, triumphantly plucking the checkout card.

"And you're three days overdue, so that will be only thirty cents. You're a lucky young man."

In fact, I felt very lucky as I strolled out of the library for the last time. My life of crime was finally over.

Neglecting One's Hobbies

Every organizer of a support group, a volunteer club, a study session, a sports team, or a committee shares a certain realization with other organizers: volunteers would rather not attend meetings.

During business hours, it is impossible to attract much of a crowd for anything. Therefore, meetings of volunteers must be held in the evening. The evenings of choice invariably exclude Friday, it being the traditional party night or stay-at-home night. For the same reason, weekends are totally out. Monday nights are risky, too, the day itself being so traumatic.

Due to this limited weekly window of opportunity, those of us with a significant number of interests or hobbies — call us hyperactivists — have discovered that meetings tend to overlap. They all begin essentially simultaneously, never earlier than 6:30 or later than 7:30 p.m. It is not unusual for your typical hyperactivist to double- or even triple-book meetings of volunteers.

A few evenings ago, as a matter of fact, I had four concurrent meetings. In an admittedly misguided, but Herculean attempt to please everyone, I attended one of my two Sherlock Holmes scions (promptly), excused myself early, rushed to my student inventor planning committee, slipped out the door prematurely again, breathlessly burst into the last few moments of my photography club, and then, dreadfully late and nearly exhausted, caught up with the friends of my local orchestra in time to sip coffee and enjoy the afterglow of what was apparently a well-run, productive session.

Somewhere between Holmes and Haydn, it occurred to me that my extra-curricular interests were overwhelming me. I hadn't had a dinner at home, it seemed, for two seasons. In fact, I hadn't remembered seeing any of my family for weeks.

Full of self pity as I softly dropped my second shoe beneath the bed after midnight and slid quietly between the sheets, a thought occurred to me: Millions of Americans must have similar difficulties with their respective interests. Volunteer organizations must be controlling many, many others, just as they were controlling me.

And so, as soon as I get the time, I have resolved to start a club for people just like me... people who want to shake their club-joining dependency. It will be called "Club Joiners Anonymous." Due to the fact that there is no more likely a group to join a club devoted, basically, to stamping itself out, no shortage of members is anticipated.

Consider this proposed 5-step program:

1. Admit that you have a club-joining obsession.

2. Accept the fact that, in the great scheme of things, very little will be accomplished in your lifetime by any volunteer group to which you belong.

3. Understand that you will hardly be missed.

4. Resolve to quit the least meaningful club next month and successively more important clubs each month until, eventually, your next month's calendar is bare.

5. And finally, quit my club, too.

Rituals

Oscar Levant was a world class pianist, among other things. He wasn't embarrassed to talk or write about his stopovers in mental institutions or his obsessive-compulsive rituals, as crazy as they were. In his book, MEMOIRS OF AN AMNESIAC, Levant went on at length about many of his rituals. For example, he discussed how he opened a package of cigarettes. First he counted from one to five twice over and took the tinfoil off during the latter half of the second count. If anyone talked during that ritual, he would throw the package of cigarettes away and start a new one.

Rituals are ceremonies or actions performed in a customary way. Some or most rituals reflect superstitious behavior to help create a sense of imaginary control over unpredictable outcomes.

Other famous people had rituals, too. For example, Ernest Hemingway would use his typewriter standing up. He wrote only in the morning. His motto was "done by noon, drunk by three."

Truman Capote said he couldn't think unless he was lying down on a bed or on a couch. Marcel Proust also wrote his novels lying in bed.

Victor Hugo wrote only when he was naked, so he wouldn't be able to leave his house. His valet was instructed to hide his clothes.

Hans Christian Anderson carried a coil of rope wherever he went for fear of being caught in a hotel fire.

William Faulkner typed with his toes instead of his fingers. Can I make this stuff up?

Mary Shelley had a domesticated 23 foot long boa constrictor that she draped around her shoulders while she wrote.

Ezra Pound preferred to breathe through his nose, except when writing, when he would breathe exclusively through his mouth.

William Wadsworth narrated every poem to his dog. If the dog barked, he would revise the poem.

Henrik Ibsen worked at a desk with a portrait of his arch-rival, playwright August Strindberg.

Balzac drank 50 cups of coffee a day. Balzac died of heart failure, by the way, at age 51. Don't try that at home, boys and girls.

Charles Dickens ran a comb through his hair hundreds of times every day, all day long.

Friedrich Schiller could write only in the presence of the smell of rotting apples.

Beethoven's breakfast was strong coffee, which he prepared himself with great care: 60 beans per cup, which he personally counted every morning.

Tchaikovsky believed he had to take a walk of exactly two hours a day and that if he returned even a few minutes early, great misfortunes would befall him.

Sigmund Freud's wife put toothpaste on his toothbrush each day to save him time. Imagine being that crazy guy's wife.

Alexander Graham Bell kept his windows permanently covered to keep out the harmful rays of the moon.

Professional athletes are notorious for practicing rituals. If an athlete believes in a ritual, he expects it to help him. Of course, the ritual works, if at all, only when the person believes it will. If a random player is told to tug on his ear before swinging a bat, for instance, it wouldn't have any effect. But to a player who considers that action to be good luck, the ritual could make a difference.

Retired major leaguer Kevin Rhomberg was an exceptionally superstitious outfielder. If anyone touched him, he would have to touch him back. He also refused to make a right turn on the diamond. If he had to go to his right to make a play, he would spin in a circle.

Tennis star Serena Williams wears the same pair of socks throughout a single tournament. Ms. Williams also bounces the ball a specific number of times during a match — five times before a first serve, two times before a second serve. Watch her next time she's on T.V.

Michael Jordan always wore his UNC trunks under his Bulls uniform.

Celtics guard Jason Terry's underwear superstition forces him to wear the shorts of his opponent's team to bed the night before a game. He says this helps him get in the mindset of his opponents. I believe him.

Retired pitcher Turk Wendell insisted numbers in his contracts ended in 99, his jersey number. He also would eat four pieces of licorice during games and would brush his teeth in the dugout in between innings.

Blackhawks hockey player Stan Mikita's pre-game ritual was to flick a lit cigarette over his left shoulder before taking the ice each night. I suppose his teammates learned where to sit or stand when he was scheduled to play.

In between periods, late Flyers goalie Pelle Lindbergh insisted on drinking a particular Swedish beer called Pripps and would drink it only if there were two ice cubes — no more, no less — in his glass. It had to be hand-delivered by the same trainer every night.

Portuguese professional footballer, Cristiano Ronaldo, has to make sure his right foot touches the grass first before stepping onto the field for a game.

Tiger Woods decided that red was his winning color before he went pro. So he wears red shirts every Sunday.

Rafeal Nadal, a national tennis player for Spain, has to have all of his water bottles lined up with the labels facing the baseline of the tennis court.

Before every game, Minnesota Timberwolves forward Kevin Garnett bangs his head on the basket stanchion. Ouch.

Wimbledon champ Goran Ivanisevic would always make sure to be the second person to get up from his chair during a change over. Then he made sure not to step on any of the lines while walking back onto the court. Between matches, the day after a victory, he would do everything exactly the way he did it the day before — which included wearing the same clothes, eating the same food, and talking to the same people.

Corey Perry, the star winger of the Anaheim Ducks, performs an eight-step ritual before every game that includes twirling his stick a certain way and tapping the ice before going into the locker room to put his pads on.

I don't know about you, but those stories make me feel more normal.

Remembering the First Time

When it comes to food, my brain is pretty impressive. I don't have to tell you, because you have one, too. Standard issue. But indulge me for a minute and think about your brain and mine. Not only can our brains figure out problems, coordinate our bodies, and get us through the day, they also have a memory that can simply amaze us.

For example, I was walking down the street at lunchtime last week when I had an urge for a slice of pizza and a Coke. I can remember when and where I was when I purchased my first Coke in a bottle from a dispensing machine.

It was at a gas station around the block from where I lived in Flushing, New York. When I bought my first Coke in 1954, the standard Coke bottle was six and a half ounces. That was plenty big for a six-year-old, and I remember that neither my friend Paulie nor I could finish a whole bottle by ourselves. But we gave it our best try. Must have taken us 45 minutes to drink half of our respective bottles.

When I moved to upstate New York 27 years ago, a local restaurant advertised, "all the chicken wings you can eat," for $4.95. Since I loved chicken, this sounded like a wonderful opportunity. Buffalo chicken wings were just making their way out of Buffalo, but I hadn't heard of them.

It was about 6:00 p.m. on August 28, 1983. I arrived at the restaurant and was seated.

"Is this really true?" I asked the charming young waitress. "I can have as many wings as I want? Seriously?"

"Yes, sir" she said. "When you finish a plate, I will bring you another one and another one, until you are full. Would you like yours hot?"

Now, remember, I had not heard of the Buffalo hot chicken wing revolution sweeping the country at that time. I figured that if I didn't order them hot, they would arrive cold, which was not appealing.

"Of course I want them hot," I said, tucking my paper napkin into my shirt. "Extremely hot."

They arrived on a very large platter, an unnatural shade of red and steaming hot, as I recall.

"Yum," I'm sure I said out loud while subconsciously rubbing my belly.

I bit into the first wing and felt my esophagus implode. My mouth was ablaze with spicy heat. I drank half my glass of water in three gulps.

I stomped over to the hostess desk and demanded to see the manager of the restaurant.

"What are you trying to pull here?" I blustered. "Your sign says 'all you can eat chicken wings' and when I get here, I find that they're inedible. What sort of scam is this?"

The manager extended his profound apologies, but they weren't adequate for me. I stormed out of the place in a huff, my mouth still burning, vowing never to return.

Now, 31 years later, I can still remember the incident and my first taste of Buffalo hot wings. I have had many opportunities for chicken wings in the ensuing years and I often order them, the hotter the better. But that first time was such a shock to my system, I'll never forget it.

I look forward to my next culinary adventure, knowing that it may earn a permanent place in my memory. But I sure hope it will not bump the memory of something truly important, like the first time I tasted coffee ice cream.

Oh, that was July 14, 1955.

II

DOCTORS AND DOUBT

A Disease of My Own

I have a lot of medical problems. I live in hope that I will develop a unique disease that someone will name after me.

Most diseases are named after the physician or scientist who first described the condition, usually in an article in a respected medical journal. But occasionally, a disease is named after a patient. Those are called eponymous diseases. A well-known example is Lou Gehrig's disease. Although Lou Gehrig, a New York Yankees player in the 1900s, was not the first patient who contracts amyotrophic lateral sclerosis or ALS, the association of such a prominent person with the then little-known disease resulted in his name becoming associated with it.

Valentino syndrome was named after the actor, Rudolph Valentino. That syndrome is for pain presenting in the right lower quadrant of the abdomen caused by a duodenal ulcer with perforation through the retroperitoneum. Easy for me to say.

Some fictional characters have diseases named after them if they displayed characteristics attributed to a syndrome. These include Miss Havisham syndrome or Diogenes syndrome, named after a Charles Dickens fictional character, Miss Havisham, in GREAT EXPECTATIONS. Plyushkin syndrome was named for a Nikolai Vasilievich Gogol's character. It is applied to people who collect and amass various useless things, a behavior known as compulsive hoarding.

To be an auto-eponymic disease, the individual whose name is being used must have been either affected by the disease or, preferably, to have died from it.

In 1906, Howard Taylor Ricketts discovered that the bacterium that causes Rocky Mountain Spotted Fever is carried by a tick. He injected himself with the pathogen and was rewarded with his name on the disease rickettsiosis. In a related story, Ricketts didn't die of Rocky Mountain Spotted Fever; he died three years later while investigating typhus in Mexico City.

The so-called Thomsen's disease is an autosomal dominant myotonia of voluntary muscles, described by Julius Thomsen about himself and his family members. So not only did Julius spread the disease among his family, but he got to name the disease for himself. Nice guy.

Peruvian medical student Daniel Alcides Carrión inoculated himself with *Bartonella bacilliformis* in 1885 and came down with what we now call Carrion disease.

Here are some well-known diseases named after the doctors and scientists who discovered them.

Alzheimer disease was named after Alois Alzheimer and Early-onset Alzheimer disease also named after Alois Alzheimer.

Barlow disease, related to scurvy due to a lack of Vitamin C, was named after Thomas Barlow, not to be confused with Barlow's syndrome, named after John Barlow, which is a valvular heart disease.

Crohn's disease, a type of inflammatory bowel disease, was named after Burrill Bernard Crohn, a gastroenterologist, in 1932. So it's been around for a long time even longer than its name has been around: 85 years. There are no medications or surgical procedures that can cure Crohn's disease. So if you're looking for a hobby, you might consider curing Crohn's and perhaps getting the cure named after you, like the Jonas Salk polio vaccine. Many people will thank you, I'm sure.

Harvey Cushing named Cushing's disease which is a cause of Cushing's syndrome characterized by increased secretion of adrenocorticotropic hormone (ACTH) from the anterior pituitary. He also named Cushing's ulcer, a gastric ulcer associated with elevated intracranial pressure. For goodness sake, don't confuse Cushing's disease or Cushing's syndrome or Cushing's ulcer with ectopic Cushing syndrome, which occurs due to exogenous steroid use.

Graves' disease was named after Robert James Graves. It's an autoimmune disease that affects the thyroid and — I think the medical phrase is — makes your eyes bug out.

James Paget was pretty prolific, as diseases go. He came up with Paget's disease of bone, which is the excessive breakdown and formation of bone, followed by disorganized bone remodeling. He also named Paget's disease of the breast, which has nothing to do with bones, hopefully, but is a type of cancer that outwardly may have the appearance of eczema, with skin changes involving the nipple of the breast. He also named Paget's disease of the penis, a rare form of cancer, and Paget's disease of the vulva, also a rare, slow-growing, noninvasive adenocarcinoma in the skin. So you see, James Paget was responsible for a sort of organ of the month club of diseases.

Tourette syndrome named after the person with the longest name I've seen a long time: Georges Albert Édouard Brutus Gilles de la Tourette.

Baron Munchausen was not a physician or scientist, but he lent his name to Munchausen syndrome, a factitious disorder wherein those affected feign disease, illness, or psychological trauma to draw attention, sympathy, or reassurance to themselves. Patients with Munchausen syndrome do not really believe they are sick; they only want to be sick, and thus fabricate the symptoms of an illness. I can relate to that one. Munchausen syndrome by proxy is when a caregiver fabricates or exaggerates health problems for the person she's caring for, with the primary motive of gaining attention or sympathy from others.

I spent an enjoyable hour reviewing diseases on the Internet that I've heard of. You wouldn't believe how many, many more obscure diseases and syndromes are named after people. I counted more than 400 on a Wikipedia web site of eponymously named diseases.

But I haven't come across a Mark Levy disease or a Mark Levy syndrome, so there's hope for me. Perhaps someone can diagnose the disease of a pathological desire to share silly Internet-derived trivia with public radio listeners. Boy, doesn't *that* have my name on it.

A Perfect Storm of Silence

I used to live on Florida's Biscayne Bay northeast of Miami. The blue water is populated with small and large motorboats, which I classify as noisy and noisier. At night, some of the boats have lights and horns. Let me rephrase that: some of the boats have lights; they all have horns.

Churches are nearby, competing with their clanging bells for parishioners to attend social functions or, on Sundays, to pray for better health and more money.

In the early evening, wispy clouds glow purple and gold, like broad, supernatural brush strokes on a larger-than-life canvas. It provides an idyllic backdrop for a never-ending row of airplanes, barely spaced apart and periodically buzzing over my head on their final approach to Miami International. It's a familiar sound to me and I never used to think about it.

One early morning last week, I walked onto my balcony, expecting the usual barrage of discordant sounds, many from objects that I couldn't see, but I was met with a perfect storm of silence. No sound met my ears: not the usual, raucous sound of gardeners and their lawnmowers and weed trimmers and leaf blowers, not the bellowing of sanitation men competing with the mechanical din of garbage trucks, not the car and truck engines and motorcycles and power boats. I heard no traffic, no horns blowing, no doors slamming, no neighbors shouting to each other, no cell phones ringing and ringing and ringing; not even the siren of an emergency vehicle could be heard. (This *is* Miami, after all.) No airplanes flew overhead with their crescendoing roar. No birds flocked, squawked, or chirped. No wind whooshed against my windows. Hushed were my dishwasher, my washing machine, my vacuum cleaner, my asthmatic refrigerator and its ice maker, and my indispensable air conditioner.

This had never before happened to me.

The preternatural silence was... well... preternatural. As I took in this uncanny phenomenon, like a colorful movie without dialogue, music, or sound effects, it occurred to me that I might have slept through a thermonuclear war. I might have gone deaf during the night. Or I might have been teleported into some bizarre Twilight Zone episode. After all, crazier things routinely happened on *The Twilight Zone*.

Remember, Helen Keller, the blind and deaf author and advocate for people with disabilities? She was asked about not having senses of sight and hearing. She said, "Of all the senses, sight must be the most delightful." Yet surprisingly, she wrote, "The problems of deafness are deeper and more complex, if not more important, than those of blindness. Deafness is a much worse misfortune."

So here I was, standing on my balcony and, for all intents and purposes, unexpectedly as deaf as Helen K.

Curiously, I found the experience not frightening, but actually pleasurable, as if I had entered an enchanted, three-dimensional, still life painting. Without sound, the world appeared as still as a snapshot, even though sailboats in the distance moved slowly, like tiny cue balls over a giant, felt pool table. They were so far away, in fact, they seemed to be moving in slow motion, adding another aspect to this other-worldly event.

Few places on our planet can afford us absolute silence. Even our overhead electrical wires provide a hum. But on a memorable camping trip in northern Canada years ago, I got to see the Northern Lights cascade across a midnight sky in soundless undulations. The show was eerie, exactly because of its lack of accompanying sound.

Now back to Florida last week. I walked the length of my balcony as quietly as I could, not wanting to break the spell and spoil the moment that engulfed me.

The view evoked absolute tranquility, but with crystal clarity, reminding me of times I'd hiked in the Rocky Mountains where the air was so pure, trees and brooks and mountains looked like high-definition photos. Near and far objects were all sharply in focus. Just like that time in the freshest air, I didn't want this time in total silence to end. But like a great novel, I knew it couldn't last forever.

And then suddenly with a rush, all of the noises of nature and civilization returned, crashing into my skull. First a lawnmower ramped up, followed by a macho kid on the water gunning his motorboat engine, and finally a sanitation crew banging empty trash cans 20 feet away. I was jarred awake from my reverie. As Ekho, the Greek god of sound, is my witness, I was physically forced to retreat two steps.

It's difficult to know how every noise-making device within earshot conspired to be silent for those few minutes. If I knew how to reproduce the effect, believe me, I would love to.

Theoretically, every air molecule could move to a corner of your room, but the chances are astronomically great that they won't. So it is with the curtain of silence I experienced. Like a hole-in-one on an empty golf course, I just know it will never happen again.

All I have left from that occasion is the memory of a surrealistic dimension, as Rod Serling might have said, a dimension not only of time and space, but of blissful silence.

Ain't Enough Seasons

Woody Allen was once quoted as saying that when he was playing jazz clarinet, he wanted to be writing a screenplay; when he was writing, he wanted to be directing a movie; and when he was directing, he wanted to be editing. Whatever he was doing, he'd rather be doing something else.

It's that way with me and the seasons. I'm always looking forward to the next season. When it's winter, I can't wait for spring. Well, doesn't everyone? But when it's spring, I want summer, and when it's summer I want the fall.

I don't know why I'm preoccupied with the season that's always just around the corner. It's certainly not because I want to be older. And it's not necessarily because I'm uncomfortable with the present season. I mean, what could be better than spring for sunshine, fresh fruit and skimpy wardrobes?

Lately, I've noticed that thinking about the next season isn't enough for me. I'm starting to project two seasons ahead. In the middle of the summer, when it's a hazy, hot, and humid 98 degrees, I'm fantasizing about a winter blizzard. Even I, as detached from reality as anyone, realize that that's just crazy.

Frankly, I'm more than a little concerned that my desire for future seasons may not stop at only two seasons in advance. I can see the time when I'll be pining for, say, the fall, when it's only winter. To outsiders, it may appear that I'm nostalgic for the season just passed, but I'm really looking *forward* three seasons.

You can see how dangerous this line of thinking can be. I'll be only one small step from hoping for the very season that I'm in. What will happen then? I'll be both happy when I look forward to my season, and sad that I'm already in it.

It's like being halfway through a hot fudge sundae. The hot fudge (i.e., summer) eventually cools, while the cold ice cream (i.e., winter) is melting. No wonder so many people enjoy the seasons and the promise of the seasons. Too bad there aren't more of them.

Amorous Birds

Scientists tell us that birds don't chirp, cheep, beep, chatter, and sing purely for our benefit. For many birds, those sounds represent mating calls. If a bird hears a particularly sexy tune, she may check out the originator with a view towards, you know, starting a family and a nest. So bird melodies are basically an audible equivalent to singles want ads in the local newspaper.

For better or worse, we humans don't rely exclusively on the sounds of our voices to influence potential mates. We have opposable thumbs, remember, and cork screws for wine bottles.

Unlike the mating habits of humans that seem to peak on Thursday, Friday and Saturday nights, at least in my neighborhood, birds reach their romantic apex seven days a week and always in the morning. Early in the morning.

In upstate New York where I live, birds can't wait to get started. In the spring, when my windows are open to the beatific (bee-ah-TIF-ic) sounds of nature, the first cute coloratura creature lets out a tentative beep around 5:00 a.m. By 5:15, a couple of dozen of the little oversexed, ornithological darlings are singing to beat the band and, by the way, to wake me up.

If birds had evolved with opposable thumbs, I might be sleeping in, more often.

Occasionally, I try to imitate the sounds I hear — at least the simple ones. But birds don't seem to be fooled. They don't respond. They're just too smart for me, I guess. Just as well. I wouldn't really want to lead a little puffin on, romantically. It could never work out. There would be no future in it. That sort of relationship would probably be illegal, anyway.

I once spent a couple of days and nights in Charlotte, North Carolina. I noticed that libidinous, egg-laying, feathered vertebrates exist there, too, but they don't get started until much later, after 6:00 a.m. More civilized, I think, but still a long way from "Divorced male, 50, financially secure, seeks open-minded gal, 18-24, for trysts at the No-Tell Motel. Please send photo."

Another Medical Breakthru

I visited one of my many doctors a few weeks ago. He is my main doctor, what those in the health industry call my primary care physician. At this point, all of my doctors are younger than I am. In fact, I graduated from law school at about the time my primary was learning the complexities of "The Itsy Bitsy Spider."

But I don't call these medical youngsters by their first names. I call them "doctor." They seem to appreciate that and it really doesn't take much to keep them happy. All I have to do is stay sick but, of course, not too sick. The game is over if I die. This is my responsibility: to linger as long as possible, helping them in a small way to put their kids through college and make their car payments.

My primary physician has an office that curves around a bend on the fourth floor of the hospital I visit. Inside the curve are nurses' stations. (You don't need to know that, but one of my listeners wanted more detail in my stories. Hope you're happy now, Marge.)

"Your tests are back, Mark," he said.

I could tell he was pleased. "I've been taking my meds faithfully, Doc," I said. "How am I doing?"

"Actually, quite well. Indicators show your stress level is much lower. Your blood pressure is down. How are you sleeping?"

"Great," said I.

"Digestive issues?"

"Not anymore."

"Headaches? Memory loss?"

"Not that I can remember," I said. "Everything's improved. That prescription you gave me must be working, huh?"

"I have to confess something to you," he said.

I learned forward in my seat. It's not every day that a doctor confesses something. This was going to be good. I was so excited, I might have rubbed my hands together.

"The medication I prescribed was a placebo."

"Well, whatever it is, I think I should take a higher dosage. It's really working."

"No problem at all," Doc said. "It has no medical viability. It's an inert sugar pill to fake you out into believing it causes a reduced stress level."

I was astonished. What a revelation. My primary was playing with my head, manipulating me to believe something that wasn't true. And I bought it. Was I that weak-minded?

Now that I've thought about it, I guess I am. I'm very susceptible to TV ads, for example. That tells you something. If one of those luscious pizza ads appears on TV — you know the ones that show such a crusty crust, creamy tomato sauce, and melted, stringy cheese, you can almost smell it in the room — I cannot go to sleep without ordering a pizza.

So I went home and Googled "placebo." Here's what the online dictionary said: "a usually pharmacologically inert preparation prescribed more for the mental relief of the patient than for its actual effect on a disorder; any dummy medication containing no medication and prescribed to reinforce a patient's expectation to get well."

The placebo worked so well on my health, I decided to try it out on my car.

When I ran out of windshield wiper fluid recently, I opened the hood of my car and found the reservoir and I went through the motions of adding fluid to it. But the container I used was empty. Then I slammed the hood down with a flourish, so my car would think all was well.

Need air in my tires? Not so fast. A quick trip to the gas station, removing the air fill cap, and a fake pump of the compressor and hose, and I was on my way, my car no wiser for the experience.

Back left blinker light bulb out? You got it. Just a removal of the lens and a tweak of the same old, burned out bulb would do the trick.

And so it goes.

Yesterday, my car limped into my car dealer's service center for its 20,000 mile checkup. The manager came out half an hour later and for a minute I honestly thought he would give my precious automobile a clean bill of health. But no, he had an impressive list of things he had found and an estimate of $540 to fix them all.

Now you might think I would have been upset, but remember, my stress level is down. I toyed with the idea of unleashing another set of placebos, but I think my car has begun to catch on.

I figure the repair bill is still cheaper than a trip to my primary. Now if only I can get Blue Cross/Blue Shield to cover it.

Autumn is the Noisiest Season

When I moved into my present house a few years ago, I would have thought that summer would be the noisiest season, with my neighbor's compulsion to start extremely early on weekend mornings, fiddling with his loud, gas-powered lawn mower and electric hedge trimmer and mulcher and shredder and who knows what-all. The guy has a love affair with any form of the internal combustion engine.

Then there's the lightning and thunderstorms to rattle the fillings in my teeth. And how could I ignore the rhythmic chirping of crickets and the buzzing of other unseen, but vociferous insects?

Or maybe the noise would be greatest, I thought, in the winter when the beautiful silence associated with pristine blankets of snow is rudely punctuated by incessant, staccato blasts of my neighbor's snow blower, near and far, and near again.

When the snow isn't too deep, he drags out his chain saw to cut wood, ostensibly for backup fuel if he runs out of gas; but when the snow is deeper, I am most happy to hear the blissful cacophony of snowmobiles that superimpose his sounds.

The spring, of course, carries with it the din of tillers and clippers and pruners and barbeque contraptions being assembled with every known hyper-resonant metal tool. It is this season that my neighbor embarks on home projects evidently requiring huge quantities of custom-made beams of lumber that can be created only with electric saws, electric planers and battery-powered hammers. Mufflerless motorcycles and sports cars also hit the road on crisp mornings, before the dew evaporates, adding to the cumulative sum of vibrations of my neighborhood.

But none of those irritating sounds compares to autumn in my neighborhood. I'm not talking about my neighbor's annoying motorized leaf blower or his amateur hunting party unlawfully trudging over my property before the sun rises, accompanied by 100 decibel observations and suggestions and commands and humorous anecdotes. They are strident, but at least short lived.

I'm talking about surviving in nothing less than a war zone. You see, stately, large oak trees surround my house. They provide wonderful shade in the summer and apparently a comfortable home for birds in the spring. But in the fall, they also provide acorns — tens of thousands of them — falling from unimaginably great heights and impacting the roof of my house, like the continuous report of individual rifle shots.

They drop when it's windy, of course, but they also have a mind of their own, deciding to plummet randomly when they sense their time is up, day and night — especially night when I, myself, am trying to fall — asleep.

Every cloud, as we know, has a silver lining. In my cloud's case, the barrage of acorns helps drown out the delicate but incessant racket of field mice preparing their winter encampment in my attic — beneath the acorn storm and above my bed every autumn.

Coming to My Senses

Quick! How many senses to you have? I'll get you started. There's the sense of sight, the sense of smell. Go ahead, count them up. I'll wait.

Did you come up with five senses? Boy, are you off. That was the original number of senses identified by Aristotle two thousand three hundred years ago.

You probably overlooked your sense of thirst, your companion sense of hunger, and the opposite: your sense of fullness of your stomach.

You also have a sense of balance and acceleration, scientists call equilibrioception, and your sense of pain, called nociception. And for what it's worth, you may have a good sense of direction.

You probably have a sense of body and limb position, called kinesthetic sense or proprioception.

Some people have a better sense of time than others. And some of us have a sense of fatigue that only an afternoon nap can satisfy.

Scuba divers may have an acute sense of pressure. But I'll wager most divers don't experience a sense of drowning too often.

Thermoception is a sense of relative temperature.

How about a sense of itching? I don't know what that's called, but you sure feel it when you're interviewing for a job, right?

I hope you have a sense of need to urinate from time to time, closely related to a more general sense of urgency.

If you look forward to *Weekend Radio* every week, you must have a sense of humor or at least a sense of amusement. Some of the more philosophical parts of *Weekend Radio* might appeal to you if you have cultivated a sense of values. Or maybe not.

Scientists have identified some 20 senses, believe it or not, but that's not nearly enough for me. I have many other senses.

For example, I sometimes have an overwhelming sense of desiring hot pizza loaded with mozzarella, spicy tomato sauce, and a crunchy crust. Maybe that should be called "pizzaception."

I often experience a sense of curiosity about what certain movie starts look like in their underwear. I should call that sense, "pornoception."

I had a definite sense of foreboding the first time my teenage daughter borrowed the family car. I call that "autoception."

I also had a sense of dread when a family member was offered a credit card for which I was asked to co-sign. Call that "creditception."

I've experienced a sense of tender, true love a few times already in my short life. I call that "cupidception."

I imagine there will be quite a sense of euphoria when I win the lottery, but (alas!) I can only guess at what that sense of incredible wealth feels like.

I've had a sense of failure in any number of situations; taking a driver's test for the fourth time comes immediately to mind. Which reminds me: I have a heart-stopping sense of fear when I see a police car, emergency vehicle lights aflashing, in my rearview mirror. That doesn't happen so often anymore, now that I've figured out how to use my cruise control.

Waking up in a hospital room surrounded by medical personnel frowning and shaking their heads has stimulated my sense of illness or injury.

Very often I try to fight the feeling that I may be the only person in the room who knows what equilibrioception means. That feeling, I'm proud to admit, is a sense of superiority. Now you can have it, too.

Contagious Yawns

When I see someone yawn, I can't help myself. I yawn, too. At the risk of putting some of you to sleep, I want to talk about yawning.

I don't know exactly what survival value this phenomenon of infectious or contagious yawning may have, but it's widespread enough to spawn a number of studies. About half of us start to yawn when we see someone else do it, or hear someone do it, or even if we think about it. And we're not the only species that yawns in response to another's yawning. It turns out that chimpanzees yawn when they see other chimps do it and at least some species of dogs yawn when they see a human yawn.

When it comes to catching a yawn, I'm about as susceptible as they come. As I said, I yawn when I see someone else yawn. No exceptions. It can be a man or a woman or an infant, old or young. When they start to yawn, I'm already yawning to beat the band. I can't suppress the urge to yawn even when I see the word in print. Y-A-W-N. See, here I go again. [YAWN]

To illustrate my over-the-top reaction, which is way above the response of most people, I have to go back a few years, when I lived in Massachusetts. You know about Boston accents, in which words that have an "a-r" are pronounced with a flat "a" and barely a hint of an "r." The famous example is, "paahk the caah in Haahvaahd Yaahd." When I lived up there, native Bostonians called me "Maahk."

I got used to that accent after a while, but I happened to be listening to a call-in radio show one afternoon in my caah. The topic for discussion had to do with home-made clothing, knitting and crocheting in particular. A woman called in to announce that she was having problems finding a store that sold the type of yaahn she needed to make a caahdigan. Even though I knew she was referring to yarn, I couldn't resist yawning when she mentioned her local yaahn store. She used the word about 20 times in a three-minute monologue and, by golly, I yawned 20 times.

The Y-word wasn't the only reason I eventually moved from Massachusetts, but it was certainly a factor.

I hope I haven't bored you with these observations. If I have, do what you have to do, but please cover your mouth.

Contraindications: The Game

I thought of a new game. I call it *Contraindications*. Here's how you play it: I list one or more possible adverse side effects of taking a particular medication and you tell me the name of the drug. A contraindication is a symptom or condition that makes a particular drug, procedure, or surgery inadvisable. Absolute contraindication means that the substance could cause a life-threatening situation. Relative contraindication means that caution should be exercised when two drugs are used together. This results in drug interactions. For purposes of my game, we'll just deal with side effects that might occur when a person takes only one drug.

Scientists and physicians have a whole gamut of ailments to treat, from relatively harmless but painful conditions like gout, hot flashes, and constipation to the potentially fatal, like seizures, diabetes, and cervical cancer.

Sometimes I can't figure out what an advertised medication is intended to cure, but the contraindications are always explicitly stated. They're unmistakable. I got some of the clues for these drugs from T.V. commercials and others from the Internet.

Let's start my game off with a simple example: what medication can cause permanent, partial blindness, dizziness, drop in blood pressure, headaches, and upset stomach? I'll give you a hint: the advantages may be worth the risk. Answer? Cialis for erectile dysfunction. Now with the more popular Viagra, you risk, in addition to permanent, partial blindness may also be chest pain, nausea, and facial flushing. But isn't a satisfying sex life worth a touch of blindness?

For the second question, what medication can cause persistent fever, bruising, bleeding, paleness, fatal blood disorders, or serious infections like tuberculosis, and nervous system disorders such as multiple sclerosis, seizures, or inflammation of the nerves of the eyes, or cancer? Here's another hint: a second drug for treating the same condition can cause numbness, swollen face, and lymphoma. A third drug to treat the same condition can cause gastrointestinal hemorrhages and, well, death.

In this example, you get extra points for identifying the ailment. The drugs are, respectively, Enbrel, Humira, and Celebrex. They are all used to treat arthritis.

But the granddaddy of contraindications for arthritis is Vioxx. Its side effects include stomach and intestinal bleeding, serious kidney problems, hepatitis, jaundice, tiredness, itching, anxiety, blurred vision, colitis, confusion, depression, fluid in the lungs, hair loss, hallucinations, insomnia, palpitations, pancreatitis, ringing in the ears, and worsening of epilepsy.

Boy, if you can run that gauntlet of medical infirmities, you deserve to have your arthritis pain lessened. I think arthritis sufferers must be the bravest patients in the world, willing to risk even death to have their condition treated.

A certain medical condition has a number of medications for treatment that can result in chest pain, digestive problems, ulceration of the esophagus, inability to stand or sit upright for 30 minutes, and bone pain. The condition is osteoporosis and the treatment culprits are Actonel, Boniva, and Fosamax.

How about this one? You can risk sudden or severe changes in mood or behavior, like feeling anxious, agitated, panicky, irritable, hostile, aggressive, impulsive, severely restless, hyperactive, overly excited, or even suicidal, in an effort to treat what ailment? Ironically, it's depression and Paxil and

Wellbutrin are the medications. So if you are depressed, these medications can solve your problems by provoking suicide. Logical, I think, but extreme.

Anemia is a serious condition, as we all know, but you might think twice before taking Procrit to treat it, since you could be subject to hypertension, seizures, thrombosis, stinging, bruising, itching, headache, indigestion, heartburn, diarrhea, constipation, sneezing, coughing up blood, darkening around your mouth or nails, dizziness, fainting, blurred vision, slow or difficult speech, loss of memory or ability to concentrate, seeing things or hearing voices that do not exist, floppiness or loss of muscle tone, blood clots in your heart, legs, or lungs, wheezing, difficulty breathing or swallowing, or hoarseness. I don't know all the symptoms of anemia, but I'll bet they don't hold a candle to the potential symptoms of the Procrit treatment.

Finally — and I bet you thought this would never end — what ailment can be treated with medications that can result in headache, diarrhea, abdominal pain, constipation, upset stomach, vomiting, cough, cold symptoms, dizziness, and rash? And what are two of the medications for treating that condition? The condition is heartburn or indigestion and the meds are Nexium and Prilosec.

I hope this new game has helped you decide whether you want to risk treating your ailments when, as Sir Francis Bacon observed, the remedy is worse than the disease.

Effexor is Stressful

For a number of years now, I've been taking Venlafaxine, whose brand name used to be easier to remember: Effexor. Those must have been the days before the patent owned by Wyeth ran out. Now it's marketed by Pfizer. I'll continue to call it Effexor. It's a serotonin-norepinephrine (nor-epi-néfrin) reuptake inhibitor (SNRI) antidepressant. Don't worry; there won't be a test on this today.

Effexor was developed for reducing anxiety and even for lessening the effects of OCD or obsessive compulsive disorder. Let's face it: couldn't we all use a little less OCD in our lives?

The drug's efficacy, as we say in the medical biz, is similar to or better than sertraline, which you may know as Zoloft; and fluoxetine, which your parents may know as Prozac.

Effexor was prescribed for me by a psychologist who thought it would help me reduce stress and, until recently, it's been efficacious. In fact, it's the most important capsule I take every day. I feel grouchy when I don't take it. Worse yet, the people around me can also tell when I don't take it.

"Did you take your chill pill, today?" my wife will ask when my patience with her is starting to wear.

So Effexor, for me, is the good news.

But I happened to Google the drug and discovered excess serotonin activity can produce a spectrum of specific symptoms including cognitive, autonomic, and somatic effects. The symptoms of an overdose may range from barely perceptible to — I was alarmed to learn — fatal. Yeeks!

Surpisingly, though, the general fear of an overdose isn't what's causing me stress. It's something more specific that happened last week.

See, I have this plastic pill organizer I fill once a week with all of my vitamins and medications. I highly recommend it for recovering OCD sufferers.

Filling the contraption is a bit of satisfying work once a week. It saves me time the other mornings. I just pour the pills out into my hand, careful, (*careful!*) not to drop any of them. Then I transport them carefully to my kitchen table so I can take them with breakfast.

But last week, after I placed my usual English muffin on the table and as I sorted my pills prior to swallowing them two at a time, like a big boy, I discovered that my little Effexor capsule wasn't there!

Now this wasn't like me. I distinctly remember loading my organizer a few days earlier with all of my pills. Yet the capsule was missing. I was beside myself. What if this wasn't the only day I was about to skip my Effexor? What if I hadn't loaded a capsule in each compartment in the rest of my pill organizer? What if, despite my ultra-careful handling of my pills, I had dropped some of them, including my chill pill? What if I had run out of Effexor altogether and hadn't ordered a refill? What if I was losing my mind, thinking I had accomplished other things that I actually hadn't? What if my whole life was unraveling and, like with so many other things, I was the last to know?

Luckily, I discovered a supply of Effexor in my prescription vial on a shelf in my medicine cabinet, alphabetically placed, of course, between my Vitamin Ds and my fish oil. So with shaking hands, I carefully removed a single, slippery capsule of the precious medication to replace the missing one, returned to the kitchen with the elusive item clenched firmly in my hand, and finished breakfast, still lost in thoughts of contingencies.

It wasn't until I cleared the table after breakfast that I realized the original Effexor capsule had rolled under my plate, in some cruel game of pharmacological hide and seek. Disaster averted. Whew!

Ironically, the very medication that was supposed to relieve anxiety that day caused me even more stress. The moral of this story is, when you can't find your chill pill, just chill out and go back to bed.

False Memories

As I age — and tell me if this happens to you, too — I tend to forget things, like what I was looking for when I entered my bedroom and how many children I have. But I understand that sort of thing happens to almost everyone. The phenomenon that has started to concern me is the opposite: I remember events distinctly that, well, never happened.

The events in question involved my friends, so I like to believe it is *they* who have forgotten the details of these events, due to their advancing ages.

But I will let you decide for yourselves. Here are three incidents that I swear happened just the way I will relate to you, regardless of denials by the other person involved. In fact, I'd be happy to take a lie detector test. That's how sure I am.

Here's the first: About 20 years ago, my friends Alan and Kathy invited me to stay overnight with them in Chicago, since I had a business meeting there. In the morning, Kathy prepared a lovely three-cheese omelet with spicy onion and chili sauce that she called a Mexican omelet. It was so good, in fact, I recreate the dish every month or so at my own home ever since. By the way, Alan had left for work early that morning, so I have no witness that Kathy served that Mexican omelet to me. As luck would have it, Alan and Kathy visited me at my home a few years ago. To impress them, I made a superb Mexican omelet.

"Wow," Kathy exclaimed. "This is delicious. I'd like the recipe!"

"Hey," I replied. "It's *your* recipe. Don't you remember?"

"I never had this in my life," she protested.

So there you have it. One of us was lying. But it couldn't be me, could it? I mean where else could I have learned the recipe?

Here's example number two: About five years ago, my friend Ken had tea and cookies with me and suggested, instead of sugar or Sweet & Low, I should try an herb called stevia. "Just as sweet," he said, "and totally natural." I went out and bought stevia in a product called SweetLeaf. He was right. It's an excellent, no calorie sugar substitute.

When he came to visit last year, I served him tea again and offered SweetLeaf.

"What's that?" he asked. I told him it was stevia and, would you believe it? He gave me a blank look.

"You know," I said, "the natural herb-based sugar substitute you told me about."

There was no recollection at all. In fact, he wrote down the name of the plant and the product, so he could get some when he returned home.

So that's two out of two. Ready for the last one? When my friend Sue's children were toddlers, she gave them frozen grapes. It was a healthy alternative to ice cream, she said. Now, some 20 years later, her kids all have graduate degrees. When I whipped out a bowl of frozen grapes and offered her some, she thought they made a nice snack and wondered how I had thought of that.

As much as I hate to admit it, folks, I'm just not that creative. I wouldn't have invented a Mexican omelet, or frozen grapes, and I wouldn't have known about stevia on my own. But here are the very people who introduced me to these things denying that they ever did.

Notice what all of these incidents have in common: detailed memory, on my part, of people, places, and things; no witness; and complete denial by the perpetrators. The odds that one person would have not one or two, but three delusional friends, defies logic, I know.

But whom are you going to believe? Those three unreliable narrators you've never met or me, a guy who woefully lacks the imagination to make this stuff up?

Fear of Just About Everything

I don't always look up interesting topics on the Internet. Honest! Sometimes a web site finds me. For example, the other day I was minding my own business when a web site called phobialist.com came to my attention. To be truthful, I may have provoked the event by googling "fear of running out of topics for *Weekend Radio*." In any event, I now have a list of about 600 phobias in alphabetical order. I'd like to share some of the more obscure phobias with you and leave the mundane ones for another day. No need to talk about fear of floods, fear of wet dreams, or fear of vomiting on an airplane right now.

Did you know some people have a fear of frogs? That's called betrachophobia. You can have a fear of being tickled by a feather, in which case you're pteronophobic, spelled with a "p." I suppose you might have a fear of being tickled by a frog, in which case you'd have betracho-pteronophobia, which is easy for me to say when I'm not being tickled.

Looks like many people have fears of other people. For example, you might have a fear of young girls (parthenophobia), a fear of teenagers (ephebilphobia), or a fear of old people (gerontophobia). So you can move easily from one fear to another as your relatives outgrow your fear of them.

For every occupation, there seems to be a fearful word. If you're afraid of your dentist, you have dentophobia. See how easy this can be? And if you must walk to your doctor's office across a side of town inhabited by beggars and hobos, I hope you haven't developed hobophobia. I once had a dentist with breath like a hobo's, but luckily for me, I didn't have hobodentophobia.

Scared of foreigners? In general, that's xenophobia, although there are separate words for fear of the French, the English, the Chinese, the Greeks and, of course, the Germans. You might know these words if you attended more parties. That wouldn't be easy if you're an enochlophobe, fearing crowds or mobs.

There's always a silver lining: if you avoid crowds, you won't be visiting the circus, so your coulrophobia, fear of clowns, won't act up.

Some people fear childbirth, which I believe is entirely understandable, but I wasn't aware there are actually four words to identify that phobia: maleusiophobia, tocophobia, parturiphobia, and lockiophobia. Those are run-of-the-mill childbirth phobias. But if you're unusually concerned about delivering a deformed baby, you've graduated to teratophobia.

One of my favorites is the word that means an irrational fear of chopsticks. It's Conseco-taleophobia, which seems harder to say than to use the darn things, but then again, I'm no psychiatrist.

If you suffer from enissophobia, you may decide not to be an essayist for *Weekend Radio*, because enissophobia is the fear of criticism — not that Robert Conrad would ever criticize anyone.

Here's another cutie: the fear of everything. It's known as panophobia. That's not exactly what I've been developing myself — a fear of phobias. Oh wait. There's a name for that, too. It's phobophobia.

You can find all these and more online, if you don't have cyberphobia, a fear of computers, that is. The web site is called phobialist.com.

Forbidden Fruit

Imagine you've just bought a sports car that can easily reach 140 miles per hour, but the speed limit on the interstate is only 65.

Or how about owning a stereo system in your apartment in which the speakers are capable of breaking your living room windows, but the home owner's association limits your volume and the time of night you can listen to music.

Have you ever traveled to an all-you-can-eat buffet just to discover all the prime rib has already been consumed?

These are just some of the frustrations we face in modern America.

Here's another frustrating scenario taken from my own pitiful life.

I'm cruising down the supermarket aisle looking for goodies that my lovely wife, the former trauma nurse, tells me are absolutely no good for me. In fact, she says, they'll kill me eventually. I just know she'll throw out whatever I take home.

Why do I bother shopping at all?

My pantry and freezer used to be filled with items that I'm not allowed to enjoy.

I could purchase Oreo cookies with double stuff chocolate filling, but I can't eat them.

I might have all the makings for a thick, rich, Ben & Jerry's Cherry Garcia ice cream soda, but I can't even make it, much less drink it.

I could buy six brands of expensive, imported brie cheeses, but I'm forbidden from placing them where they belong, on the Ritz crackers that were discarded last week.

The bakery section of my supermarket is simply outstanding. It offers fresh bread, muffins, cakes, pies, and elaborate desserts. Basically, I'm not allowed even to visit that section under penalty of amputation, dismemberment, and death, not necessarily in that order.

Remember Mallomars? Chocolate-covered marshmallows on a graham cracker you could freeze or have them at room temperature? I found them online, but it turns out they're also poison. Who knew?

I used to love licorice — especially the chocolate ones — but not anymore.

I have beer and wine and aperitifs for before my meals, but the meal always seems to get to me before I have a chance to imbibe.

Likewise for after dinner drinks. I have a dozen bottles, but somehow I never get to sample them after my dinners.

All of my choices have too much sugar, too much salt, or too many carbs.

So this is my dilemma, my personal tragedy. Do I continue to buy forbidden groceries, knowing how exasperating it will be to see them thrown out in their original packages, or do I control myself at the expense of forfeiting the wonderful anticipation of consuming them, knowing, as I do, that the anticipation will never be fulfilled? Hamlet's decision was easy compared to mine.

I'll spare you from uncertainty. Yes, of course I succumb to temptation and buy the products; and yes, I fool myself on the way home from the supermarket, honestly believing the products will not reside in their respective boxes and bottles much longer, once I get my hands or lips on them. But then reality sets in and my adoring wife draws that imaginary line in the kitchen, separating me from my base instincts.

"It's for your own good," she says. "You bought some delicious things, honey, but you can't have them."

And that is where I stand. I get credit for having good taste, but no permission to take what I thought was the next logical step.

My wife has kept me alive so far, so I shouldn't complain. But it's really a shame to let that whipped cream in the Reddi-wip can go to waste.

Hurricanes and Galaxies

During the hurricane season, one morning a television commentator described one of last year's hurricanes bearing down on poor Florida's coast. He had a satellite image of the hurricane and he said it resembled another one a few years earlier. It occurred to me that I had seen a similar photo only recently.

"Wait," I said to my wife, lying in bed, feigning sleep and trying to ignore the T.V. and, of course, me. "That looks like a galaxy!"

Granted, my wife is not the amateur meteorologist slash amateur astronomer that I am, so I understood why she didn't respond with alacrity. Okay, she didn't respond at all. I trundled over to the computer and googled galaxies. Sure enough, the galaxy known as NGC4051 bore a striking resemblance to Hurricane Fran.

I noticed that NGC5055, nicknamed the Sunflower Galaxy, looks like Hurricane Gordon and NGC3031, nicknamed Bose's Galaxy, looks like just about every second hurricane I've ever seen. NGC4736, on the other hand, is a nearly perfect spiral, but it doesn't have a nickname. I think they should call it Hurricane Galaxy.

NGC5457 is nicknamed the Pinwheel Galaxy. You can probably guess what that looks like. I think astronomers are too literal. They ought to have artists name the galaxies. The Pinwheel Galaxy could be named Brenda's Migraine or maybe Crop Circle in Minnesota.

Actually, there are some mundane but descriptive names for galaxies that you may not have heard of, like the Sombrero

Galaxy, the Cigar Galaxy, the Whirlpool Galaxy, and the Black Eye Galaxy. I'd like to show you pictures of all of these, but that would dilute the excitement of radio. It's better that you imagine their shapes. Of course, you can always Google them yourself, but for Goodness' sake, please wait until after this program.

Astronomers can be semi-creative when it comes to naming their pet galaxies, but for hurricanes, the World Meteorological Organization is altogether blasé. It uses only the names of people. The WMO used to be sexist, but men's names are also used now. The names of the hurricanes sound more friendly than galaxies' names, I guess. Once a good-sized hurricane comes and goes, its name is retired. So we'll never experience another Hurricane Katrina or Andrew or Hugo or Floyd, for example. Ditto for Edna, Beulah, and Hortense. I miss Hortense already.

The center of a galaxy is called the nucleus; for hurricanes, though, the middle portion is called the eye. I suppose if you're going to name a hurricane after a person, that person ought to have at least an eye. Sounds better than the ear of a hurricane or the gall bladder of a hurricane, don't you think?

The eye is about the only part of a hurricane you ever hear about, but in galaxies, the stars around the nucleus form a disk. Those stars are called — ready for this? — the stars that form the disk around the nucleus are called "disk stars." See how uninspired astronomers can be?

I don't need no stinkin' Ph.D. in astrophysics to understand galaxies. But hurricanes? That's another story. Understanding a hurricane is, well, it's like understanding a woman.

I Like My Present Age the Most

Supreme Court Justice Oliver Wendell Holmes walked down a street when he was 90 years old or so and reputedly saw an attractive young woman. Holmes turned to his companion and muttered, wistfully, "Ah, to be 80 again."

I wonder if I will have the same wish when I get as old as Holmes was. I know a few, much younger people who already are pining for their even younger selves. That helps explain the reason many people are obsessed with looking younger. They wear fashionable clothing and hair styles and they get face lifts and tummy tucks. They listen or try to listen to rap and hip-hop music and use teenage expressions, like "omigod" and "fly girl" and "cheese" and "phat," spelled with a "p." Now if they have that sort of never-young-enough temperament, they might also wish for younger years when they hit the advanced age of 30.

If they regret reaching, say, the 40-year milestone, how will they feel when they reach each succeeding year or decade? Life must become more and more disappointing to those folks as they age. That's really too bad. It means they have less to look forward to every day. Where's the fun in that?

I, on the other hand, enjoy my present age more than I did my age last year. And last year was better than the year before. Now I'm not saying that each of my faculties is better than ever, or that there aren't more insidious signs of failing health; but I have a better adjusted attitude with each year. I have a better appreciation for how the universe works and how and why people act as they do. Now I also know better how to urge some people to react the way I would prefer, from the cashier at the supermarket to my boss. I still haven't figured out my wife, but I'm optimistic even about that, as foolish as that sounds.

I'm increasingly empowered with knowledge, and that feeling of self-sufficiency should continue to increase as I live through more events, meet more people and gain more experiences. It's a shame it will end, but I try not to think about that.

I am free not to have to prepare for events that I now know will never happen. I don't feel the urgency to rehearse with an air guitar, for example, since the prospect of rock stardom has already passed me by. And I'm not writing and rewriting my acceptance speech anymore for the Oscars or the Nobel Prize ceremony. What a relief. That saves me a great deal of time and, of course, anxiety. Nowadays, the only thing I rewrite is my last will and testament.

I don't have to practice catching fly balls to right field or get nervous about meeting my teen-aged girlfriend's parents or explain to my own parents why my 8th grade report card in Spanish isn't as spectacular as they had hoped. I don't have to stay up half the night trying to remember the capital cities of 50 states or the names of the explorers who discovered each little dinky Latin American country — information that I was pretty sure I would not need in the next 50 years... and I was right.

I spend little time thinking about what I'll be when I grow up, although I have to admit fleeting thoughts of that still cross my mind on certain Monday mornings.

Besides the obvious advantages of qualifying for senior discounts at the movies, at restaurants and at sporting events, and the deference youngsters pay me occasionally, when all of the seats are taken on the bus, here's another benefit of being older. Recently, I completed a Master Degree in creative writing. (You might not realize that from these little essays, because they are essentially non-fiction. Let's face it: you can't make some of this stuff up.) Anyway, my writing class of twenty-somethings and thirty-somethings spent time learning how to think of subjects to write about. I could have skipped those classes, because coming up with new ideas is no problem for me. By now, I've experienced all sorts of things that I can write about. I felt sorry for the younger students in my class, who could just imagine events that I had already experienced. It seemed like an unfair advantage for me, in fact.

No, compared to my earlier years, I am completely satisfied with my present age. I just wish I could somehow remember those early years better.

I'm Always Late

I have excellent reasons for always being late. First, I hate to be early. It's just uncomfortable for me to wait around for something to happen or someone to appear. I get anxious and bored at the same time. I don't know where to put my hands. Do I cross my arms or twiddle my thumbs? If I'm sitting down, I don't know whether to shut my eyes for a few moments or keep them open. And if they're open, especially when other people are in the room, where do I look? There are way too many decisions, as you can see, to risk arriving early. Furthermore, when I'm early, the party I'm meeting will be late. Happens every time.

Here's another reason I'm almost always late: I think I have more time before my appointment than I actually do. I underestimate the time needed to squeeze in another project before I'm supposed to be somewhere else. It's gotten to the point where I know how much time I have to leave for an appointment, but I decide to embark on a project that couldn't possibly be completed in that time.

If I have eight minutes before I must leave for an appointment, for example, I might begin to read WAR AND PEACE. Okay, that's an exaggeration. But if I had nine minutes.... The point is, I merely and sincerely think I have enough time to wrap up a project or two before I'm officially late, even if the project is ludicrously complex.

People, notably my wife, say that my tardiness indicates I don't respect them and their time, so I keep them waiting. I assure you, it has nothing to do about disrespecting others. I don't think I'm more important than other people, with the exception of certain relatives by marriage. No, I don't intend to keep other people waiting. This isn't some sort of infantile power strategy.

Let's face it, though: in most cases, being late by a few minutes or a couple of hours isn't going to make a difference in the great scheme of things. After all, it was only a few centuries ago that society even kept track of time to the second or even the minute. Portable time pieces — pocket watches and wristwatches — didn't appear until the early 1800s, only 200 years ago. There was simply no need for accurate time measurement before then. Hard to believe that the original Greek Olympics could be held without digital technology.

Nowadays, time pieces can measure time intervals within one part per trillion or higher. I think that's carrying an obsessive/compulsive disorder a bit too far, don't you?

The one time that it *is* imperative to get to a place on time, I've learned from sad experience, is at the airport. Airlines can be so inflexible when they don't have mechanics on strike, or equipment problems, or snow storms. And that's just another reason I hate to travel.

Medical Abbreviations

I've been spending time in my doctor's office lately, not because I'm sick or injured, but because I'm one of the few patients of his who's insured. See, he's got two kids in college and a Ferrari that is only three payments from being paid off. So he really needs me more than I need him and we both know it.

His staff is friendly enough, but after my string of monthly visits, I'm afraid they've begun to take me for granted. At least they don't make me wait in my doctor's front office like the hypochondriacs and the underinsured; but on the other hand, it seems to take him longer and longer to arrive while I wait for him, dressed only in my underwear. He keeps his examination room at a brisk 52°.

On my last visit, I began to snoop around the room, doing what I imagine most people do in the same situation: playing with the tuning forks and trying out some of his wooden tongue depressors. As I became increasingly bored, I was reminded of what Shakespeare has Pistol say in *Henry IV, Part 2*: it's an ill wind which blows no man to good. Well, the wind in his examination room was not an ill wind; it blew me to his bookcase.

A small file jutted out from the second shelf. It was labeled "Confidential Terminology." Who wouldn't be intrigued with a title like that? I knew I would never forgive myself if I didn't investigate.

But even as sanguine as I am, I wasn't prepared for the treasure trove I uncovered. It was a multipage document of acronyms and abbreviations that medical personnel use to hide information from their patients.

72

Page after page of abbreviations leapt to my unblinking eyes, alphabetical gems, one after another.

The physicians who devised this list appear to be obsessed with death. For example, if the doctor or nurse says the patient is being transferred to one floor higher than the top story of the building, it means the patient is dying. He is, in fact, NGMI — Not Going to Make It. ART stands for Approaching Room Temperature or dead. Let's face it: he's not just SIO — Sleeping It Off; he's in PBS — Pretty Bad Shape or in RBS — Really Bad Shape. The same condition is also referred to as FTD — Fixing To Die.

Sometimes, despite the best efforts of medical personnel, the patient is GDA — Gonna Die Anyway. If the patient is in that state, he may be GPO — Good for Parts Only. That's because of the presence of GRAFOB — the Grim Reaper At Foot Of Bed.

Once the patient expires and goes Paws Up because his LRO — Luck Ran Out, he is said to GTTL — Gone To The Light or HBD — He Be Dead. Discharged Downstairs means transferred to the morgue. That's very similar to Celestial Discharge or Celestial Transfer or Transfer to the ECU — Eternal Care Unit.

DOTS stands for Dead On The Spot — usually the scene of an accident. This is similar to DRT – Dead Right There. If the accident is especially violent and gruesome, the deceased is referred to as DRTTTT — Dead Right There, There, There, and There.

Beating Off Angels means performing CPR on a patient who won't survive. On the other hand, a Coffin Dodger is a person who does survive against expectations, despite the inept work of a Knife-Happy Blade — that is, an arrogant, overly enthusiastic surgeon who works in a Doc In A Box — a small clinic. He may have performed a Foreverectomy or Horrendoectomy — a surgical procedure that lasts a very long time. He may have Buried the Hatchet — accidentally left a surgical instrument in the patient. And he may have noted on the patient's record, DTMA — Don't Transfer to Me Again. Often the DTMA patients have LWS — Low Wallet Syndrome with no medical insurance or money.

If the surgeon had been more experienced, he might have performed a simple Peek and Shriek — opened the patient surgically, discovered an incurable condition, and closed the incision immediately. Unfortunately, the surgeon had no basis for Blamestorming — apportioning blame for mistakes to the lowliest medic in sight or writing SODDI — Some Other Doctor Did It.

Coffin Dodgers and other seriously injured victims sometimes spend time Gone Camping — in an oxygen tent or, if they're children in oxygen tents, Happy Little Campers. The Coffin Dodgers who are at least semi-conscious are often referred to the Freud Squad — psychiatrists.

I am happy to share these well-kept medical notation secrets with you in the hope that you may someday realize how serious your condition is and escape from the hospital before it's too late and you have OFIG — One Foot In the Grave.

Medical Abbreviations – Part 2

I mentioned recently my fortuitous discovery of a directory of doctors' slang and medical acronyms. These are physicians' shorthand to keep their observations from their patients. It turns out, acronym-wielding medicos are obsessed not only with death and near-death conditions, but also with the intelligence or, more precisely, the lack of intelligence of their patients.

A number of phrases and acronyms all refer to the same low IQ condition. We have NARS — Not A Rocket Scientist; LMC — Low Marble Count; HIVI — Husband Is Village Idiot; ERNOBW — Engine Running, No One Behind Wheel; LORNH — Lights On But Nobody Home; and DPS — Dumb Parent Syndrome.

If the person is beyond all hope, he may be referred to as Pumpkin Positive. When you shine a penlight into his mouth or ear, the light will encounter a brain so small his whole head will light up. When a patient refuses essential treatment through stupidity, he's known as Fighting Darwin. In that case, medical personnel are advised to SYB — Save Your Breath, since the patient WNL — Will Not Listen. He may also have an OPD — Obnoxious Personality Disorder. That's the type of patient who may throw an AHF — Acute Hissy Fit. Those patients are also often Bungee Jumpers — ones who pull on their catheter tubes.

And of course some patients are JPS — Just Plain Stupid when they have a self-inflicted injury involving lack of common sense. They often claim they were SOCMOB — Standing On Corner Minding Own Business when they were inexplicably injured.

Crossing the fine line between idiocy and insanity, certain patients are known as AQR — Ain't Quite Right or CCFCCP – Coo Coo For Cocoa Puffs. In extreme situations, they are referred to as having ALS — Absolute Loss of Sanity. This can help to explain elderly women who are Handbag Positive — confused and lying on a hospital bed clutching their handbag. A physician may prescribe OBECALP — "placebo" spelled backwards — to calm her. Or giving up completely, a physician may indicate TEETH — Tried Everything Else, Try Homeopathy.

When a middle aged female visits a doctor weekly just for male attention, she may be D & D — Divorced and Desperate. Sometimes she merely DIFFC — Drops In For a Friendly Chat, but physicians warn each other that she will TATT — Talk All The Time. This type of difficult patient can turn into an Albatross — a chronically ill patient who will remain with a doctor until one or the other of them expires.

A procedure has been developed for patients who overuse their call bell. It's called a Callbellectomy — removing the call bell from a patient's reach. As a last ditch effort, a nurse may dream of performing a Pillow Consult — smothering a difficult patient to be done with her.

Older patients are called Crinkly or Crumbly. If they use a walker or wheelchair, they're known as Creepers. They often linger in the Departure Lounge or God's Waiting Room — the geriatric ward.

Children range from CKS — Cute Kid Syndrome, to FLK — Funny Looking Kid, to DUB — Damn Ugly Baby. But some children have redeeming qualities like FLK w/GLM — Funny Looking Kid with Good Looking Mother. If the child requires special attention, a nurse might summon Captain Kangaroo — the chairman of the pediatrics department.

Serious injuries occur from time to time, as you would imagine, when an adversary carries a firearm. ALP means Acute Lead Poisoning or a gunshot wound, similar to a High Speed Lead Injection. Air-conditioned ALP means he's suffered multiple gunshot wounds. Transcranial Lead Therapy is when a gunshot wound passes through the patient's head.

When the trauma ward is full of gunshot and stabbing victims, it's known as a Gun and Rifle Club. If a motorcyclist is involved in an accident, he's known as an Organ Donor and his vehicle is referred to as a Donorcycle. When a patient's heart stops, it's time to use the Toaster — defibrillator.

A Silver Bracelet Award is bestowed to a patient who is a criminal, brought in by the police and wearing handcuffs. Chrome Induced Ischaemia is a patient who develops chest pains when arrested and handcuffed. Incarceritis can occur when a prisoner becomes dubiously ill when arrested.

A VIP — very intoxicated person or one who HBD — Has Been Drinking and is HTK — Higher Than a Kite or WWI — Walking While Intoxicated can FDGB — fall down, go boom and end up SIO — Sleeping It Off. An Acute Gravity Attack simply means the patient fell down with or without AOB — Alcohol On Board. Sometimes a Drinkectomy is needed to separate the patient from his beer can.

Patients who try to fake illness have what is called MGM Syndrome or ATS — Acute Thespian Syndrome — a faker putting on a good show. Sometimes a patient will have Fluttering Eye Syndrome — faking unconsciousness.

I'm glad I got to see this confidential list of medical acronyms, so I can practice my Fluttering Eye Syndrome when my doctor makes an appearance. It can come in handy when he slips on his latex gloves for the prostate exam he's so fond of.

Move Along, Old Fella

I suppose we've all been there, waiting in our car at a traffic light that turns green for us, as an elderly person — possibly the slowest moving person in the history of pedestrians — slowly, SLOWLY makes his or her way in the cross walk to the other side of the street. By the time the person has finally reached the curb, the light has turned red again.

It seems strange that the oldest people are the slowest moving. Don't they know they have precious little time left on this earth? It's time that may not even be measured in years. Perhaps hours or minutes is more like it. Now if you were, say, 110 years old and realized that the actuarial tables gave you 6 months to live, if you stayed away from fried foods, wouldn't you want to do as many things as possible in your remaining time? Wouldn't you want to sprint across the street and experience some of those things you've been putting off? Oh, I don't know, perhaps you'd want a Kobe beef steak or a shot at climbing Mt. Everest or maybe do a little sky diving? Surely you wouldn't want to spend what could be a third of your remaining life crossing the street, would you?

The younger you are, therefore, the faster you move. I think that's called a corollary. My two-year-old grandson, Solomon, tears around the house like his diaper is on fire. Sometimes he's just a blur. And the thing of it is, I don't know why he's running from place to place. The toys are pretty much identical on one side of the room as they are on the other. But boy, the speed with which he gets there takes my breath away. In fact, I'm convinced he doesn't know how to walk. When he's removed from his crib and his second foot hits the floor, he's already moving as fast as his chubby legs can propel him.

Of course, the concept of life expectancy tables is pretty foreign to a two-year-old. And heaven knows, I can't slow Solomon down long enough to explain anything to him, much less the concept of death. He has this sense of urgency, seemingly oblivious to the fact that he may well live to 125, assuming, again, that he heeds the fried foods caveat.

If you knew that you could do something now or tomorrow or next week, would you strain yourself trying to get it done immediately? I don't think so, and yet little Solomon doesn't seem to have a moment to spare. Who knows? Maybe he's trying to get important things done before he's summoned for his nap.

All I know is, if I had been in charge, I would have created people with completely opposite mobility. I would have forced young children to slow down and smell the roses, while giving old people a turbo boost of speed, so they could accomplish at least one more spectacular thing before they slowed down for good.

My Contact Lenses

I wear contact lenses. But my thoughts today aren't about the lenses themselves. They're about how they work as harbingers of my day.

As you contact lens wearers can attest, it's not always simple to get those little bits of plastic firmly seated on your eyeballs. It doesn't matter if the lenses are hard (like I used to wear), or soft (like I wear now). Either way, there are days when they just won't cooperate, sliding off my fingertip prematurely, or attempting to make a last-minute break from the prison of my eyelids.

I've discovered that, when the contact lenses are easy to insert and give me no trouble, I have a pretty good day. No one yells at me, everyone who owes me money pays me, the food in the cafeteria is delicious, and there's not a cloud in the sky.

On the other hand, I can hardly declare the same result when one or both of my contacts decides to rebel in the morning. In fact, the amount of trouble I will experience during the day is proportional to the amount of difficulty I have placing my contacts in my eyes.

The other day, for example, my right contact lens would not leave the security of my index finger or forefinger or *digitus secundus*, if you'd like to impress your friends. No matter what I did, no matter how hard I pressed the little fella against my eyeball, it remained on my fingertip, not in my eye.

Needless to say, my day turned out pretty badly. I got to my office late, I spilled my tea all over my desk, my telephone refused to give me a dial tone, and my computer began to work so slowly, it made me feel like I was Michael Phelps swimming in the Olympics.

But that's nothing compared to what happens when *both* of my contact lenses act up. On those days, it's not unusual for me to burn my oatmeal, for one of my shoes to slip off as I proceed down the stairs, for my coat to get caught on the banister, resulting in a Jerry Lewis-like descent down my stairs, and for my car's battery to need a jump.

I suppose you could draw the conclusion that, when both of my eyes can't open wide enough to accommodate my contact lenses, perhaps they're too tired from lack of sleep. It's true that I sometimes get to bed in the small hours of the morning. That lack of sleep would also explain my grogginess and ineptitude with my coat, my shoes, and my oatmeal. But what about the car not starting? How could that possibly be related to my lack of sleep?

No, I think the proof is incontrovertible: my contact lenses may not cause my woes for the day, but they sure enough predict them.

Last week, one of my contact lenses popped out of my eye as I was trying to get it in. It rolled down the side of my sink and slid down the open drain. I promptly removed the lens from my other eye, replaced my pajama top, and crawled back into bed. There's no use tempting fate.

Nap Time

At the risk of putting you to sleep faster than my essays usually do, I'm going to discuss naps, those precious intervals of sleep during the day favored by the very young and, I've discovered, many older people including me. In fact, a recent Pew Research Center survey shows that one out of three adults takes a daily nap. More men do than women.

The Internet is full of advice about the advantages of napping during the workday and how to get the most out of your napping time at the office. Someone even invented an unofficial holiday called National Workplace Napping Day, to be celebrated the first Monday after the start of daylight-saving time each spring. The theory is you need a nap on that day more than any other day of the year to make up for the hour of sleep you missed the previous Sunday morning.

I would use that logic to argue for a nap the day after New Year's Day, Thanksgiving Day, the Fourth of July, Academy Awards night, Superbowl Day, World Series Day (all seven of them), and even Flag Day for the excessively patriotic.

Of course, not all of us work in offices. Aren't hospital workers, professional basketball players, and retail sales clerks entitled to a nap, too? If you operated a jack hammer, for instance, I think you should be able to take a short nap every day, which would be a relief not only for you, but for the rest of us within earshot.

Taking a nap during the workday has a number of advantages, the most important one being an opportunity to be more productive afterwards. But if you wake from a nap feeling groggy and grumpy, as I usually do, you might feel productive even if all you do is stumble your way to the bathroom.

Here's another advantage of taking a nap when you should be working: you can make up for nap time by working late, thereby avoiding the evening rush hour, which is its own reward.

Frankly, though, as much as I appreciate workday naps, I find great pleasure also in napping during the weekend. For most of us, the weekend is for recuperating after a long week of whatever it is we get paid to do. Sometimes I'm so exhausted on Saturday morning, the first thing I do upon awakening is take a nap. That way, instead of merely sleeping in all morning I feel that I'm actually accomplishing something I can brag about on the rare occasion that I'm invited to a party that night.

Napping has been good for my marriage, too. My wife is always concerned about my wellbeing, which is why she pesters me about any number of what used to be pleasurable activities. Lethargy in front of our TV and fried chicken come to mind. Her concern for me has certainly curtailed my unhealthy behavior. But by the same token, her abnormally strong desire to keep me healthy at least until our mortgage is paid off has actually resulted in my getting out of most physical tasks from drying dishes to mowing the lawn to attending those interminable grade school music recitals. All I have to do, after beginning the activity, is clutch my heart and make a funny face and I'm excused from completing the job.

I have to admit, though, I haven't been successful at ducking all of those so-called concerts. I know what you're thinking, but the kids' performances are so dreadful, no one could sleep through them.

I'm in good company as a professional napper. Winston Churchill, Albert Einstein, and Thomas Edison advocated naps.

So did Gene Autry, the singing cowboy, and Salvador Dali. And look what they accomplished.

Business people call them "power naps," which elevates them to something more meaningful than what cats and dogs do at every opportunity. In fact, before the expression, "power naps" became popular, we used to call them "cat naps."

The Mayo Clinic also thinks they're a good idea for some people's hearts some of the time. How's that for a strong recommendation? Personally, I think that indicates the Mayo Clinic employs too many lawyers.

John Kennedy also used to take naps, or at least that's what he told Jackie. I really have to hand it to Kennedy. If Marilyn Monroe had visited me at nap time, I'm not sure what activity I would have chosen.

Not So Fat

I can't tell you how many acquaintances comment on my weight. Positive comments.

"Are you on a diet?" they say. Or, "you've lost a lot of weight."

I'm as vain as the next guy, so I can't help being flattered when I hear comments that I interpret to mean I'm skinny, but lately I've been thinking about those remarks.

Here are the facts: No, I'm not on a diet and no, I haven't lost weight.

Sure, like many people, over the years I've attempted to lose weight on diets. Some of them are known as "programs" or "clubs" or "plans"; but I can be unabashedly honest. They're simply diets. Some are balanced, some are not. Some advise me to eschew meat or fat, others boost protein at the expense of carbs, and still others claim I'll lower my cholesterol.

Almost everyone likes to think he or she is thin. It's nice to say "you've lost weight" as a greeting. It's more observant than "nice shirt" and more intimate than "hot enough for ya?"

I got an abrupt dose of caloric reality once when I met a client whom I had only spoken to. He said, "Mark, on the phone you sound 20 pounds lighter and 10 years younger."

That was nice. He managed to insult me twice in one sentence.

But getting back to compliments... a positive statement about my appearance is a reflection of the intelligence of the observer. I'm likely to think, "what a smart person," rather than "what an idiot," even if — down deep — I know the comment is false.

But wait! Maybe the person knows something I don't. I guess it's possible that I've miraculously lost weight without trying. Subconsciously, perhaps I've been choosing less fattening foods and exercising more. Perhaps I *have* been losing weight and I'm the last to know. Who's the idiot now?

I have a theory about why my appearance after some time of absence elicits comments regarding my weight. It's not only my habit of buying oversized clothing or wearing vertical stripes. It's simply the fact that the lasting impression I leave is girth. It seems to be an impression that grows over time in the mind of the observer. The longer it's been since the person has seen me, the fatter the memory of me becomes. So when we finally meet again, I appear to be skinnier than I was remembered.

Part two of my theory has to do with why I appear fatter in the first place. Simply stated, I think I smile too much. Everyone knows that when you smile your cheeks puff out. More smiling, more puffing. I'm like the blowfish of *Weekend Radio*.

So there you have it. I can appear thinner later if I smile more now. The more I smile now, the more people will eventually believe I'm thinner than ever.

Here's my next project: convincing people I used to look older.

O.C.D.

Maybe I'm crazy, but I think obsessive compulsive disorder or OCD can be a healthy thing. I'm not saying it's healthy to overdo OCD behavior. As Ben Franklin, the poster boy for over-indulgence, once said, "everything in moderation." And boy did he mean "everything."

I worked for a large company once that had what it called a "clean desk policy." What that meant was at the end of the workday, every employee's desk had to be cleaned off, and all papers had to be filed in the desk or stored in file cabinets and locked up. If you failed to obey this clean desk policy, you risked getting a sort of parking ticket from the security cop whose job it was to circulate through the building after hours, looking for stray papers. Three tickets and you were fired. I think the guy who thought up this policy had a touch of OCD himself.

Anyway, one night, at about 3:00 a.m., the security guard found one of my fellow employees walking to his car in the parking lot, turning around just as he approached his car, and re-entering the building to make sure that he had locked all of his cabinets. Apparently, he had been walking back and forth between his office and his car since quitting time, 5:00 p.m., ten hours earlier. Every time he got to his car, not being absolutely sure that he had locked all of his cabinets, he returned to double check and triple check and quadruple check. Now that's an OCD problem to be proud of.

No, I'm not advocating obsessing to a point of paralysis, like when someone can't leave his house because he's not absolutely sure that he turned off the iron. I'm talking about only a mild obsession or compulsion, or both. What harm is there in checking the iron twice before leaving the house? Or in tightening the cap on the salt shaker a second time? Or, like me, in placing your currency in order in your wallet, making sure that the fives come after the ones and before the tens, all facing the same direction and arranged in serial number order within each denomination? Does it harm anyone when I line up my vitamin bottles in my medicine cabinet in size order? Really, what harm could it possibly do to alphabetize my cereal boxes?

I marvel at other people who don't mind sorting through their boxes to locate Cheerios when, for me, it's always near the beginning of the alphabet and, therefore, on the left side of my shelf. Sometimes the position of my Cheerios box is preempted by cereals named Apple Blueberry, Apple Cinnamon, Apple Strawberry and Banana Nut, in that order, but I don't usually buy products that combine flavors, like apples and cinnamon. If the cereal tastes more like cinnamon than apples, regardless of its name, should it be stored under "C" to the right of my Cheerios? Way too confusing for those of us with even mild forms of OCD.

Frankly, I think that forcing a bit of organization on this chaotic universe I inhabit may relieve stress and perhaps add predictability to the random events I encounter every day. Not to put too fine a point on it, I wouldn't be surprised if these harmless little compulsions can even reduce global warming. Stranger things have happened, you must admit.

Of course, to tackle a huge problem like global warming, I'd have to convince many more people to pay an inordinate amount of attention to the details of their lives. Luckily, I've already seen a bumper sticker that states, "think globally, act locally." So you see, we're halfway there.

To those of you whom I've convinced today, please email me and include your phone number, so I can file away the responses in order by area code.

Olé! Extraction in the Afternoon

An encounter with the oral surgeon who intends to remove my wisdom tooth provides me with a ringside opportunity to participate in the relatively bloodless dental equivalent of a *corrida de toros, or* bullfight. My surgeon, with the unfortunate DeVriesian appellation, Dr. Payne, is the matador. And I am the bull.

Bullfights are generally held *en la tarde,* in the afternoon, as is my extraction procedure. Usually six bulls are fought, two by each of three matadors. In comparison, a patient's four wisdom teeth can be extracted in one session by one surgeon, but I elect to have only my penultimate one dispatched today.

Instead of purchasing *billetes,* tickets, for the occasion, I am expected to pay by cash, charge, or insurance form.

Dr. Payne's pleasant, air-conditioned waiting room contains a selection of magazines, which I would imagine is typically not the case for the *chiqueros,* the stalls in which bulls are held prior to their own "appointment." When I enter the room they call the operatory — my personal *plaza de toros,* or bullring — I am greeted with neither *sol* (sun) nor *sombra* (shade), but with fluorescent lights.

Like a *cuadrilla,* or troupe of bullfighters, the doctor's staff parades into the operatory, like a *paseo,* the entrance of the bullfighters into the ring, to begin preparations. One settles me in the chair and reclines it; the next attaches a cuff to my arm for continuous blood pressure monitoring; another positions a white bib around my neck like a *muleta,* or cape. Before my x-ray comes the heavy, lead-lined apron, like the *caparacón,* the mattress-like blanket that shields the horses.

Once the preliminaries are accomplished, Dr. Payne approaches me like a wary *picador,* guiding a Novocain-loaded syringe, like a miniature *banderilla,* into my gums. At this time, he performs no *adornos,* or flourishes. He is all business. I am grateful that Dr. Payne is no *novillero,* an inexperienced bullfighter. With the patience of a *diestro,* a skillful fighter, he waits for the pain-killing medication to take effect.

I lie quietly, like a confident, unsuspecting bull, trying to relax while listening to a diluted version of Barry Manilow strings, and vainly trying to imagine them to be *clarines,* the bugles used to signal the end of one act and the beginning of the next.

At this point, I can tell that Dr. Payne is sizing me up. What sort of opponent will I be? What sort of *peleo,* or fight, will I put up? And how difficult will it be to administer the *coup de grâce* to my erupted tooth?

No one can say whether a bull will be brave in the ring until the bullfight begins. A *toro malo,* or bad bull, can be unpredictable, obnoxious, or vicious. He may spring unpleasant surprises, such as *extraño*s, sudden movements. He may execute a *cabezada,* tossing his head when least desired. This, of course, can be extremely problematical, both for a surgeon and for a bullfighter *adema al toro,* who works close to the bull. On the other hand, Dr. Payne is wondering whether I am *cobarde,* a coward, who will shrink from his weapons. Perhaps (I know he is thinking), I am *un toro de paja,* a bull of straw, inoffensive and posing no danger. I believe he is correct. I am attempting to personify a *claro* — a bull that is easy to work with. I try to resonate confidence, with a demeanor of a *toro bravo,* but we both know that my blood pressure is rising steadily.

The final act of the session is about to start. He circles the chair, like performing a *veronica* or two-handed pass, smiling faintly. He instructs me to *ahormar la cabeza,* position may head, and then prepares to *cuadrar,* straighten me out for the kill. He instructs me to open my mouth and inserts not a sword, but a poorly concealed instrument that looks suspiciously like a pair of shiny pliers.

"I'll just give this a wiggle," he says, performing an *alegre al toro,* to rouse the bull's attention when the bull becomes *aplomado,* lethargic.

The next thing I know, he is twisting his hand sharply and plucking the tooth from my head, now waving it with a *desplante,* a theatrical gesture. He walks across the room, to the admiration of the *aficionados,* displaying my tooth like an *oreja,* an ear of the bull. Everyone is smiling.

Just before passing out, I gurgle a weak "*Olé*"!

Oranges

Spherical citrus fruit bearing the name of their orange color come in two major species: navel and Valencia. But using only that descriptor is like saying humans come in two major races. To a Martian, I suppose, all humans are essentially alike. Think about *that*, George Clooney. We may all look identical to a Martian.

But of course to us humans, many features and characteristics distinguish us from each other. To members of our own species, some of us are clearly taller, fatter, louder, or sexier than others. Some of us can dance, some of us can solve differential equations, and some of us can yodel. Some of us have bad breath (not to name any names, dental assistant, Marge). Some of us have better manners than the rest of us. That reminds me of the definition of a gentleman: a person who knows how to play the bagpipes, but doesn't. I wonder how that definition would translate into a Martian dialect.

I started thinking about oranges while peeling one recently. I began to consider their differences. To most of us, all navel oranges look pretty much alike, don't they? But to an orange, one navel must be as different as can be from another one. Some are darker, some are older, some are rounder, and some are smaller. Some have cancer. Some have skin discolorations. Some bounce better, some roll better. Some come from privileged families in well-to-do orchards, some are naïve, some are very dense, some speak foreign languages, I would imagine, and some are unfortunate flood victims. Some oranges have more protuberant protuberances protruding from their bodies. One may be the Jimmy Durante of oranges. Perhaps one may be the George Clooney of navels.

Florida, as we all know, is called the Sunshine State. But one of its nicknames is the Orange State. That may be because more oranges are grown in Florida than anywhere else in our country. And our country supplies about 15% of all the oranges of the world. Brazil grows more than twice as many and it has a world class soccer team, to boot. Coincidence? I think not.

It was Supreme Court Justice William O. Douglas, in the 1972 case, *Sierra Club v. Morton*, who stated that he would favor a federal rule allowing litigation in the name of inanimate objects like a valley, a river, a lake, or a grove of trees that feel the destructive pressures of modern technology and modern life. Maybe oranges feel things.

I would venture to say that, of the 5,000 oranges that a given, large orange tree can produce every year, no two are identical. They're like snowflakes in the agricultural world. Now I'm no expert. In fact, until recently, I could barely tell the difference between a Sanguinelli and a Moro Tarocco (heh heh).

If you arranged all the oranges produced in the world last year, it would encircle the planet Jupiter and still have enough left over to satisfy the Chinese army with orange juice for a month of mornings. I mentioned China because it is thought oranges originally came from that country, which begs the question, Why are the two major species — navel and Valencia — not called something Chinese? They probably *are* in China, now that I think of it.

The fact that they come in two major species is also misleading. In addition to navel and Valencia, an orange may be any of 600 types, including a tangerine, a tangelo, a Mandarin, which breaks down into Satsuma and Clementine, a Seville, a Blood, a Pixie, a Temple, or my favorite, a Honeybell.

By the way, I wouldn't repeat that statistic about encircling Jupiter to anyone, if I were you. I made it up.

Passions

Remember, "Everything in Moderation?" Right, Ben Franklin, the poster boy for bacchanalian excess. Between his womanizing and his overindulgence of food and wine, Gentle Ben certainly didn't practice what he preached. But he managed to live to 84 when the life expectancy of his fellow founding fathers was decades shorter.

So what can be learned from Ben's deeds, if not his advice? In a word, passion. Passion, the driving force that renders the most of your ephemeral stay on earth. With such a short interval between cradle and grave, you are well advised to cram as many experiences into every year — every day — as possible. Although you don't have control over the quantity of time you are allotted, you certainly have the power to control the quality thereof.

Reading between the lines, what Ben Franklin really meant to say was, "Work hard, play hard, eat hearty, laugh loudly, sing boldly, talk fast, walk fast, drive fast, read voraciously, wager recklessly, and make love with impulsive abandon, for tomorrow or soon thereafter, you will die." Let the terrifying tick tock of your biological clock, like the sound of blood pounding in your ears, be subsumed by passionate, over-the-top hyperactivity.

If life is what happens while you're busy making other plans, then frenetic, passionate activity is what can distract you as the precious moments of your life leak away. Time indeed does fly when you're having fun and, unfortunately, it flies even if you're not.

96

Grabbing for the gusto may be the most important thing you do in your brief life — a life that is more meaningful when you insert passion into the things you do, the things you want to do, and the things you have to do, the things you love and the things you hate.

Yes, there can also be a dark side to passion, as there is in so many things. The very phrase, "heat of passion" has negative connotations thanks, in part, to Perry Mason and Charles Manson. Yes, Manson and Mason dealt with extremes, but a strong inclination to dislike can be a positive force. When you really hate something or someone, be passionate about it. Hate it or them with all of your energy. Nothing is as potent as pure hatred, pure venom. Embrace the feeling, revel in the emotion.

Passion can be automatic, as in the case of those naturally enthusiastic people who live to bore you at cocktail parties with the petty, little accomplishments of their grandchildren. Admit it: you shudder, however imperceptibly, when a grandmother scrounges through her purse for the omnipresent, portable, accordion photo album.

Or the passion can be inserted consciously. It can actually be forced or contrived as Dale Carnegie and his disciples advocate. The extra effort to instill passion is greatly rewarded as you force yourself to enjoy or hate thoroughly that which you are doing.

Even the most tiresome activity can be infused with life if approached with enthusiasm, vitality, and passion. This dogma is not entirely new, of course. Evangelists have known the secrets since they learned how to propose parables. As mentioned, Dale Carnegie taught it; celebrities learn it; obnoxious sales people practice it; successful telemarketers embody it; and cheerleaders live it.

Politicians, at least in public, exude it. You, too, can turn the tedious into the terrific, not to benefit others, like your boss — although it can unintentionally have that effect — but simply to get the most from the evanescent moments that you have left of your life.

Pineapples

Quick, think of a joke about pineapples.

It's not easy, is it?

Actually, this is one instance where the Internet let me down. After much searching, I am embarrassed to admit that I couldn't find one funny joke about pineapples, and you'd think they would be crying out for humorous social commentary. Perhaps no one wants to take advantage of their odd appearance.

Sure, I found jokes about grapefruits and kiwis and mangoes and pomegranates and even tomatoes, which are fruits, even though we use them in salads. And bananas, of course. Just the word, "banana," is funny if you've drunk too much fermented pineapple juice. But I found no pineapple jokes to relate that even my four-year-old grandson would appreciate, and he laughs at everything I say.

I started doing research about pineapples. There is no consensus about where pineapples originated, although a number of countries have been proposed, including Hawaii, when it was a country, Paraguay, Thailand, Mexico, Brazil, the Philippines, and the Guadeloupe Islands in the Caribbean. A certain aged radio personality thought it might have originated in Cleveland, near a well-known radio station, but I tend to discount almost every theory I get from that guy. Frankly, he's been known to overdose on fermented pineapple juice, among other things, occasionally.

Some say Christopher Columbus got in the act along the way, transporting them to Queen Isabella, and I have no reason to doubt that, although it wasn't his most famous accomplishment.

Pineapples are awfully versatile, culinarily speaking. They are used to complement green salads and fruit salads, ham, pork chops, fried rice, pizza, fondue, and Jell-O. You can make ice cream from them, ice cream topping, sorbet, juice, smoothies, and alcoholic beverages with Spanish names.

They can be grilled and eaten by themselves or sliced into rings or bite-sized chunks and eaten with a toothpick. How's that for simplicity?

Of course, this brings up a number of questions that are probably eating you alive, like:

How do I know if my pineapple is ripe?

What are them little, ugly burrs called, the ones that are left in the fruit after the skin is removed?

How do I cut pineapples safely?

Is it dangerous to eat them little, ugly burrs?

How do I remove them little, ugly burrs without mangling my pineapple?

What purpose do them little, ugly burrs serve?

Can I place the peeled, outside skin in my garbage disposal?

Can I place them little, ugly burrs in my disposal?

What emergency steps should I take if I puncture myself while cutting a pineapple?

Do them little, ugly burrs have nutritional value?

Are there particular recipes to make them little, ugly burrs delicious?

Are them little, ugly burrs dangerous to my pets?

And probably a thousand other questions about them little, ugly burrs.

I'll tell you if you haven't guessed by now that this essay is pretty much totally about pineapples. So if you're not intensely interested in the subject, it's not going to get any better. You may want to pour yourself a glass of — oh, say, orange juice — and come back in a minute.

I have a limited amount of time now, so I'm afraid I won't be able to discuss them little, ugly burrs after all. By the way, sometimes they're called "eyes," but I think that's way too anthropomorphic, don't you?

Here's the good news: I *can* tell you how to tell if your pineapple is ripe. Smell it right at the fruit stand or grocery store. If it doesn't smell like anything or if it smells like anything other than a pineapple, don't buy it. And if you've already bought it, don't eat it. And if you've already bitten into it, you might decide not to savor the juice escaping from that first bite and flowing down your chin.

In case you have a bad sense of smell, there's another way to tell if your pineapple and you should become one. If you can pull off one of the leaves from the very top of the pineapple without much effort, the pineapple is ripe. Hmmmm. Then again, it could be rotten.

Peeling a pineapple can be tricky. The important thing is not to cut yourself with a sharp knife and avoid being gored by the thing. In a way, that's pretty much the same advice I give to aspiring bullfighters.

Saving Time on Envelopes

In 1963, the U.S. Post Office, now called the United States Postal Service or USPS, decided to simplify our lives — or at least Post Office employees' lives — by introducing two-letter abbreviations for the 50 states. This was to accommodate a seven-digit field for zip codes, too, which were introduced the same year.

Some of the abbreviations are difficult to remember, since a number of them begin with the same letter. For example, the words, Michigan, Mississippi, and Minnesota all start not only with M, but M-I. Who knows how many residents of Michigan have received threatening reminders from companies intending to harass customers in Minnesota or Mississippi.

The two-letter abbreviations make sense for states that have the same starting letter, like the eight M states and the eight N states. But I now live in Florida and there's only one F state, just as there is only one G, H, L, R, and U state. There's also only one P state at this time, but when Puerto Rico becomes a state, Pennsylvania will lose its status, at least abbreviation-wise.

Of course, I am going along with this silly naming convention, even though only one letter would be sufficient for Florida, but it's starting to bother me that I have to use the letters FL for my address when, in fact, there would be no confusion if I used just the letter F by itself. I can't help thinking how much effort I've put into adding the superfluous second letter so many, many times.

If you multiply my frustration by the 19 million of my fellow sunshine state residents, you can see how astonishing our efforts are. If each person who lives here writes or types a

Florida address only once a week, for instance, the amount of wasted ink or printer toner can amount to well over two, maybe three gallons every year. In this age of conservation, that certainly appears wasteful, don't you agree?

Well, if you do agree, perhaps you'll like my plan: let's all write to the USPS and ask it to change its policy for Florida. When the USPS receives millions of requests, it's sure to capitulate.

I know what you're thinking: wouldn't the effort be ironically counter-productive if we included the second letter of the postal abbreviation on our return addresses? Glad you asked that insightful question. And you're right: sometimes you have to travel in the opposite direction in order to get where you want to go. At least that's the way I saw it when I spent last weekend in Georgia.

Senior Discounts

In general, it's not particularly pleasant to get older. One often loses his health, his hearing, and his hair. It becomes more difficult to get up from a chair, tie one's shoelaces, and move quickly. Sometimes it becomes difficult to move at all, now that I think of it. One's memory for people, places, things, and family member names also fades with age.

In *Henry IV*, William Shakespeare referred to an ill wind which blows no man to good. You may know the more modern aphorism, "Every cloud has a silver lining." And so it is with age.

Depending on your age, you may qualify for all sorts of discounts that younger folks can't obtain. This is a valuable advantage for people who look their age or older.

Senior customers are defined as those over 65 in places like Boston Market, Hardee's, Taco Bell, and Alaska Airlines, which saves you 10% on flights to places you may not wish to visit most of the year.

But you don't have to wait until you're 65 for a discount at places that classify people as seniors when they reach their 62nd birthday. These businesses include Amtrak, Greyhound, Marriott hotels, and Bally Total Fitness, where you save $100 on a membership if you promise not to break a bone on their exercise equipment. White Castle will sell you 100 hamburgers for the price of only 90, which is quite a bargain if you still have your teeth. And the National Park Service will sell you a lifetime pass for only $10 believing, I guess, a lifetime deal isn't going to amount to much at your age.

Some places choose the age of 60 to separate young people from the rest of us. For example, at Ben & Jerry's you can get 10% off your ice cream sundae. Hyatt Hotels can save you up to 50% on their rooms. And Applebee's gives you 15% off your check. That's like the restaurant has decided to pay your tip. Mrs. Fields is happy to break off 10% of the price for her cookies. Great Clips and Super Cuts give small discounts to 60-year-olds who want a haircut. That may be because there's so little hair to cut once you acquire snow on the roof.

Discounts abound for people as young as 55 years old, too. Jack in the Box gives those younger seniors a whopping 20% off the final bill. Maybe I shouldn't have said, "whopping." But speaking of Burger King, you have to be 60 years old before you get a 10% discount there. At 55, though, KFC will throw in a free small drink — not literally, of course — with any meal.

"How about 50 year olds," I can hear you ask, now that I'm on a roll. There is something for everyone once you hit the half century mark, you'll be happy to learn. Krispy Kreme, for example, honors your age, if not your waistline, with a 10% discount for everything it sells. Kmart takes 20% off its items. Steak 'n Shake is good for 10% off on Mondays and Tuesdays. SeaWorld Orlando and Busch Gardens Tampa both slice $3 off one-day tickets. As long as it's Tuesday, the Plant Shed nursery will prune 10% off your bill, too.

I'll share a secret with you. I've been visiting many of these fine establishments for a few years now, even before I reached my present advanced age. The discounts are rarely advertised. You have to ask for them. I approach the person behind the counter — and he or she is usually a teenager — and I say in a quaky voice, "Do you have a discount for seniors?" I'm well past the age of embarrassment to ask for it, which is yet one more advantage of maturity. If a discount exists, the counter kid tells me what it is.

Sadly, no one has ever asked for proof that I'm 50 or 60 or even 65. I believe that's because, to a teenager, everyone over 30 looks ancient. And it just wouldn't be polite to question the honesty of a person as old as his grandmother.

When my father turned 74, he told everyone he was 75. "You see," he confided to me, "people respect me more at that age."

Now I'm thinking that, like me, he had other intentions when he devised his plan.

Sooo Skinny

Last night I had a nightmare. I dreamt that my latest diet had actually worked and, in fact, that I had lost many, many pounds. I was a shadow of my former self. When the wind blew, I tumbled down the street like a thin piece of paper caught in the whoosh of a leaf-blower. A door opened and I was sucked in to my favorite restaurant. The dessert cart came by but I ignored it. (I told you this was a nightmare.)

I woke up halfway through the dream in a cold sweat. Unfortunately, I drifted back to sleep. I found myself standing in a large theater, among the audience. A comedian on the stage watched me try to find my seat.

"What's your name, honey?" he asked. Apparently in my dream I had changed genders, too.

I looked around like I didn't know whom he was talking to. That was the only real part of the dream, I think.

"Yes, you, Ms. Dental Floss," he said. The audience began to titter.

"I'm Virginia," I answered, choosing the longest name I could think of.

"Well, Virginia, you're awfully thin. One could even say skinny."

"You can never be too skinny," I replied smartly.

"Hey," said the comedian, "you know you're too skinny when you have to run around the shower to get wet."

I could feel myself blushing in my dream. Apparently that was exactly how I took my showers.

"Are you staying in this hotel, honey?"

By now, the spotlight had migrated from the stage to me in the audience. I nodded sheepishly, like a skinny woman caught in the headlights. The audience laughed for no reason. It sounded suspiciously like the canned laughter from the old *Bill Cosby Show*.

"Well," the disembodied comedian's voice continued, "I'll bet you can see out the peephole with both eyes."

The audience erupted. I turned to look around me.

"Hey, honey. Don't do that. When you turn sideways you disappear."

I faced the stage again. It was dark as a tomb, but less cheerful.

"Wow, look at that, folks," the comedian's voice said. "She has to stand in the same place twice to cast a shadow."

I just wanted him to stop, but he obviously had more ammunition stored like a paranoid squirrel. "Is it true," he said, "you had to take in the dress you stole from my daughter's Barbie?"

I was reeling.

He went on: "I heard you could lie under a clothesline and not get a sunburn."

By now, I had had just about enough of this abuse. I sat down on some fat dude's lap. I have to admit, it was pretty comfortable. I was learning how mortifying it was to be a thin person. But the voice wouldn't stop.

"When you swallow a meatball, Doll," he said, "do you think you're pregnant?"

More canned laughter. I was humiliated. All I wanted was to be blissfully fat again.

I could finally feel myself coming out of my dream, thank goodness. I promised myself I would never diet again. In fact, I had an overwhelming urge for a five-scoop, hot fudge sundae.

But I could still hear the comedian's voice chasing me from a great distance.

"Don't worry if you start to drown in the hotel swimming pool, Babe. I'll just toss you a Cheerio...."

Cheerio for now from Mark Levy, now fully awake.

Taste Versus Texture

When it comes to food, taste isn't everything. Maybe it's because I'm getting older and my taste buds are dying faster than pretzels disappear at a Superbowl party, but I've discovered so many other qualities of food and drink that, to me, are at least as important as taste.

For example, if hot chocolate isn't piping hot, I'm not interested. Ditto for pancakes and french fries. I know some people who claim to like day-old, leftover pizza, but as far as I'm concerned, the words "pizza" and "cold" should never be used in the same sentence. After all, part of the fun of eating pizza is trying to avoid burning the roof of my mouth. There's no challenge eating it cold.

Who was the genius who invented hot fudge sundaes? I hope he or she made a bundle of money. It's well deserved. My pleasure is directly proportional to the heat of the fudge.

On the other side of the temperature scale, it's important that beer be served almost frozen, preferably in chilled glasses or mugs. Warm beer is about as appealing as feeling hot air from my broken air conditioner blow on my face.

The wrong temperature is not the only factor that can make a perfectly good thing bad. Take crispness. If a potato chip is soggy, I don't care how good it tastes. I just can't have more than one. I've noticed that cold cereals start out crispy but rapidly get soggy in milk, so I've learned never to answer my telephone once I start on the puffed wheat.

When something like popcorn is supposed to be crispy, only crispy, crunchy, crusty, or crinkly will fill the bill. Certain foods should be noisy. On the other hand, I can't ingest hard donuts or hard bagels. I'm tempted to donate them for use as targets to the local skeet shooting range. Corn bread, to be great, should be warm, sweet, and crumbly, all at the same time.

Cookies are unique. They're ambi-textural. If I expect one to be soft and chewy, it better not make a noise when I bite it, especially at a long, boring wedding ceremony. But if a cookie is supposed to be hard, I want to see crumbs fly across the room like shrapnel.

I don't neglect my sense of smell, either. If whipped cream smells like sour cream, I'll pass on whatever it's adorning. Turmeric is pretty nasty. I once got some on my hands and couldn't get rid of the stink for two weeks. There are exceptions to noxious odors; in cheese, for instance, and garlic bread, the smell doesn't deter me from gobbling some up. But nothing, really, should ever smell like sardines.

Celery, crisp. Peaches, juicy. Bread, warm. Mashed potatoes, smooth. Chicken soup, hot. Cinnamon buns, sticky. Clam chowder, thick. Is that too much to ask?

If the texture isn't what I'm expecting, I may never get to the taste, which probably disappoints my remaining old, tired taste buds. But what have they done for me lately?

The Life of a Food Taster

Recently, as I lay in bed trying to recover from a horrendous upset stomach and high fever due to an otherwise delicious lunch, I started to think — hallucinate, really — about food tasters. You know, those fellows in Rome during the first century who tasted every meal the emperors were served before the dinner bell rang.

The most famous taster was Halotus (20 A.D. – 70 A.D.), a servant to the Roman Emperor Claudius (10 B.C. – 54 A.D.). It turns out that Halotus may have acted at the behest of Claudius' wife, Agrippina the Younger (16 A.D. – 59 A.D.). She was the sister of Caligula, by the way, which has nothing to do with this narrative.

So Halotus poisons Claudius with mushrooms so that Agrippina's 16-year-old son Nero (37 A.D. – 68 A.D.) from a previous marriage can take over the "emperorcy." This conspiracy theory is bolstered by the fact that Nero, when he ascended to the throne, executed many, including even his mother.

However, he did not execute Halotus or even fire him from his position as food taster. Nero may have been one of the worst tyrants in history, but at least he didn't dispatch his food taster.

A food taster's job is to make sure no one poisons the boss. This is why I think being a food taster is a pretty cushy job. In addition to the enviable opportunity to taste every meal the emperor is about to eat — the food probably being a notch or two better than the gruel the average slave is served — the food taster is virtually assured that nothing will happen to him. How incompetent would an assassin have to be to attempt to poison a monarch knowing that the trusty food taster would raise the alarm himself by dying first?

I don't think an actuarial study has been performed, but I'll bet the life expectancy of a taster rivals that of a teetotaling vegetarian.

I had thought that the occupation of food tasting went out with Romulus Augustus — or Romulus Augustulus, for short — the last Roman emperor whose reign lasted not quite a year. But no, even recent U.S. presidents have food tasters. Although the Secret Service won't admit it, presidents from Reagan to Obama take people they call White House chefs along to sample the vittles whenever they travel from the White House.

I don't know if the Pope has a food taster, but isn't it suspicious that you never see His Holiness with a corned beef sandwich or even an ice cream cone in public? What's up with that?

The Power of Suggestion

I am a pushover to the power of suggestion. I'm incredibly weak-willed when it comes to advertising messages.

If I see a television commercial for pizza, for example, I simply cannot relax until I order one.

Boy, are those pizza commercials alluring: rich red sauce, creamy melting mozzarella cheese, crispy crust. I can almost taste the oregano. It is so easy for me to transform that slight urge to an obsession. In fact, I lose the ability to concentrate all afternoon until I've burned the roof of my mouth on a slice.

But it is ice cream that's really my downfall. I see 31 flavors parade across the screen in gorgeous colors, overflowing their ice cream cones.

And it's all I can do to control my impulse to order one of each, especially the flavor of the month, which usually appears rich and nutty and absolutely irresistible beneath a thick layer of steaming hot fudge and a cumulus cloud of whipped cream.

Some of the little things, the little fattening things, like sugary doughnut holes, make me want to jump through my TV set and grab them out of the hands of infants.

On the other hand, I can't say that watching exercise routines on the screen stimulates me to take up those activities. I rationalize that the people on those commercials are merely actors, paid to say their lines and show off their abs. Until someone is willing to pay me to disrobe and smile while riding an instrument of torture, I don't think I'll be buying one. How's that for restraint?

The Shortest Memory

One of the many, many complaints of older people is their failing memory. With few, but enviable exceptions, most of us don't have the memory we used to. We forget names and/or faces of actors, athletes, acquaintances, friends, and even relatives.

We can't think of the word that's on the tip of our tongue. Searching for our missing keys or eyeglasses or hearing aids is a daily, frustrating activity.

How often have you entered a room to find you can't remember why you traveled there? We have to look up phone numbers that we used to know by heart. Sometimes the phone number we can't remember is our own. We can't remember the T.V. program or the magazine from which we learned an interesting fact. We can't remember if we took our medication today. We can't remember when the service guy will come to fix our cable. Worst of all, for me, is my inability to remember the punchline of a joke.

In addition to measuring memory loss, scientists have focused on our attention spans, which apparently go hand-in-hand with memory. A great deal of effort (and government funds) has been expended to learn about human memory and attention spans. One researcher found that technology has significantly lowered the average attention span of teenagers. The attention span of a child or teen who is actively trying to pay attention is 3 to 5 minutes for every year of the child's age. As a result, a 13-year-old has an attention span between 39 and 65 minutes. So remember that fact when you start to lecture your children. Brevity may be the best strategy when you try to get your points across to that teenager of yours.

Scientists also have experimented with animals to discover the limits of their memory and their attention span.

Fruit flies suffer memory deficiencies analogous to those seen in human Alzheimer's patients. Aβ-associated memory loss has been investigated in fruit flies, with their little brain cells expressing the Aβ-42 peptide, which is a specific version of the protein comprising 42 amino acids, seen in Alzheimer's plaques. These fruit flies are models of the Alzheimer illness because the Aβ-42 is encoded by a human gene inserted in their genome.

Scientists have developed behavioral experiments for fruit flies, if you can believe it. Lord only knows who designs those experiments for the itty bitty fruit fly. I have a mental image of a fruit fly scurrying around, trying to locate his eyeglasses.

I was encouraged to learn that squirrels remember only 20% of the places they've stored nuts for the winter. I think I can remember where I placed a jar of cashew nuts at least 50% of the time, making me much better at this game than the average squirrel.

Sheep, on the other hand, are intelligent creatures with good memories. Someone discovered that sheep can remember as many as 50 faces for 2 years and specific individuals for even longer. Researchers tell us that sheep retain the memory of an absent flock member for years, which is impressive when you realize that all sheep pretty much look alike.

Crows also remember individual faces over long periods of time. They can communicate information about people to other crows. One reason crows have exceptionally good long-term memories might be a function of excellent eyesight, coupled with a lack of intrusive activities and thoughts. We humans deal with cell phone and football game interruptions all the time. But crows? Not so much.

Rats and mice have a memory that researchers can measure with the use of mazes. Remembered smells and even feelings can also be measured, apparently. The rodents have better memories than camels, which must make camels feel badly. After all, camels already feel inferior to horses. Now they can't even measure up to mice, memory wise.

The animal with the shortest memory is the common goldfish, who cannot concentrate for more than 3 seconds. But they are able to recognize time, which is more than you can say about me when I'm doing something interesting.

Some researchers believe it's not the goldfish that has the shortest memory span, but hamsters. Try to remember that when you visit your local pet store again.

The Weather

Weather forecasting, as we all know, is not an exact science. In fact, even using the words "weather forecasting" and "science" together is oxymoronic.

Yet we have a fascination with the weather, a fascination that goes beyond preoccupation. It borders on an obsession. The space devoted to weather in newspapers and the Internet rivals only the space for astrology. It seems like half of the local evening news is spent talking about the weather, and not only what the weather will be tomorrow, but predictions for the day after, and the day after that. The local weather folks have the temerity to predict how nice or lousy the weather will be a week from now, right down to the exact temperature. They certainly sound like they know what they're doing. Who can argue with predictions as precise as 52 degrees or three to four inches of snow, spoken so confidently, so authoritatively?

Weather broadcasters like to be called meteorologists, which adds to their credibility, they think. That's a big step from what we grew up with: "weather girls." Nowadays, many of the broadcasters aren't women, anyway.

After a drink or two, most folks in the weather biz will confess that accuracy of predictions deteriorates dramatically with time. In fact, their predictions three days out are generally less than 60% accurate and predictions five days out are less than 40% accurate. In other words, five-day forecasts are not accurate about two times out of three.

I lived in Denver for a while way before I moved to Colorado again, recently, and always enjoyed watching the weather segment on local TV. Not because I believed in the forecast, but because I was intrigued to learn the reason yesterday's forecast was wrong. These meteorologists would spend up to half of their allotted time explaining why their prediction didn't come true. Most often in Denver, the blame was placed on the Rocky Mountains, which the weather people kept forgetting to take into account. Hello? It's the Rocky Mountains!! How could you miss them?

In Michigan, they blame the Great Lakes. In Texas, it's the Gulf Stream. They don't have to blame anything in Honolulu or San Diego, since the weather is pretty much the same every day; and in any case, as my friend's father used to say, sometimes even a blind chicken finds the corn.

In my present location at the center of the universe in upstate New York, I get a kick out of the discrepancy between national weather and the local weather forecasts. The national networks show weather maps that may clearly indicate wind, rain, sleet, snow, or hail the size of watermelons. But the local weather prophet says something like, "it will be a gorgeous day today with plenty of sunshine." Don't the local folks watch the national news? Shouldn't they at least look out their window now and then?

But getting back to accurate weather forecasts, what constitutes accuracy, anyway? Does the actual high temperature of the day, for example, have to be exactly what was predicted? The answer is no. Studies of accuracy usually have some wiggle room, like plus or minus three degrees. So if the forecast predicts a high temperature of, say, 70 degrees and the actual temperature reaches only 68 degrees, that's still considered an accurate prediction. I have no problem with that.

Weather guys have figured out a nice way to hedge their bets. They say things like, "there's a 60% chance of rain," or "it will be partly sunny." And when they are clueless, they blame it on the weather itself: "The weather will be unsettled tomorrow," they may say, like it's the weather's fault we don't know what it will be. It's hard to argue with those sorts of statements, but it's also hard to make plans based on them.

I understand that forecasts arouse passion if they're at the extremes. You know, we tend to perk up when we hear that the blizzard of the century is heading our way or we're due for 27 inches of rain tomorrow. When such extreme predictions don't come true, most people are happy. If six inches of snow were predicted and we receive only two inches, we usually don't get mad at the weather folks. People are more upset when only two inches are predicted and they get dumped on.

What bothers me most, though, is not when the weather folks predict good weather and they're wrong. That may be inconvenient, if I forget my umbrella or mittens, but it's not disastrous. It's the opposite situation that disturbs me. When a day is supposed to be terrible and it turns out to be beautiful, I get agitated. I wonder how many people cancel their plans — their picnics, their days off work, their trips to visit friends and relatives — based on the erroneous predictions.

I'm not saying that predictions are intentionally wrong or that there's a better way to predict the weather than the computers and satellites we use; but it strikes me that if the rest of us did our jobs as poorly as meteorologists, more airplanes would fall out of the sky, more nuclear power plants would explode, and more éclairs would be only half-filled.

If Robert Conrad did his job as poorly as my local weather forecaster, for example, he would be fired and you wouldn't get to hear my rantings, unless you came to visit. If you do plan to visit me, by the way, here's a bit of advice: please don't pay attention to the weather forecast.

Too Late for Child Prodigyhood

I wanted to write fiction, but lacked sufficient motivation. So a few years ago, shortly before my 60th birthday, I applied for a master's degree in creative writing. The program was low residency, meaning only one week attending classes on campus per term; the balance of instruction and writing exercises via my computer, accessing the Internet and communicating with professors by email. A number of colleges and universities offer this sort of program and creative writing programs appear to be some of the most popular.

In the course of that education, I completed the first draft of my first novel — the school calls it a thesis — which was in good enough shape to earn the degree, but neither good enough, in my opinion, nor long enough to submit to a publisher.

My novel is a near-future science fiction thriller, reminiscent of Michael Crichton's works. That is, the premise or "hook," as we say in the writing biz, could happen today or tomorrow, much like the events of *Jurassic Park* could conceivably happen today, especially the scene of the lawyer being eaten by a T-Rex. Originally, I planned to write a happy ending, but I soon learned it is almost impossible to make the future seem interesting without some cosmic disappointment or entropic disaster. So I succumbed to Crichton's technique of having future technology kill or maim a number of people.

As for the publishing aspect itself, self-publishing an online novel seems to be more fashionable than ever for authors, especially first-time authors. In many ways, it is more convenient, and, for the majority of us newbies, an alternative to the almost impossible undertaking of penetrating the publishing industry. For me, though, self-publishing still has a stigma, an illegitimacy, like a first-time mother forsaking the pleasure of 18 hours of hard labor and delivering a baby the easy (easier?) way, by Caesarian section.

As you would expect, my perspective of the writing and publishing process is somewhat different from that of my 20-something year old classmates. For example, writing a best seller does not have the same degree of commercial significance or career importance for me, as I have a relatively secure day job as an intellectual property lawyer. By the way, I was one of only a few in the audience who saw the movie version of *Jurassic Park* and refrained from cheering during the above-mentioned T-Rex feeding scene.

In the last 30 years, I have published my fair share of non-fiction. If United States patents count, I have over a million words in print. I have also submitted articles to various magazines about law, movie making, music, Sherlock Holmes, left-handedness, and even orchids. I have written essays for the Mensa *Bulletin* and letters to literary journals and newspapers, from the *Bulletin of Atomic Scientists* to the Binghamton *Press*. I have given dozens of lectures to corporate clients, high school and college students, and government and community service organizations in many states on a number of topics, usually relating to patents, trademarks, or copyrights.

I am also a contributing editor for *Videomaker* Magazine and sit on the editorial board of the esteemed but obscure *Journal of Irreproducible Results*. In addition, I am a regular contributor of essays to the National Public Radio show, *Weekend Radio* with Robert Conrad, a program that is aired in upstate New York, Little Rock, Cleveland, Knoxville, Honolulu, and Kalamazoo, among equally prominent places, I am proud to say.

While some of the pieces I have created arguably could be considered more fiction than truth, the fact is I have not published a single fiction story, much less a novel, so far. Sadly, I have noticed, there is precious little opportunity to use dialogue in a patent application.

In a way, then, I am approaching the field of writing as a serious hobby — pleasurable and life affirming, but not essential to my survival. That is both a blessing and a curse. I have little sense of urgency and I am under less stress than the typical first-time novelist who I imagine makes a conscious decision every night about what dinner he can afford.

Perhaps that's my problem, plain and simple: I am not a starving or even a hungry artist. I do not seem to have the requisite fire in my belly that, say, Norman Mailer had when he was 25 or James Jones had at 22. Since I lack the struggle to provide for my basic needs, it seems I am also close to the tipping point of inactivity.

Professional writers often advise young, would-be authors that nothing short of fulltime effort can result in success. In my case, so far they are correct. I cannot expect to produce a best seller until I actually complete a manuscript. And a 150,000-word manuscript, I am finding, is difficult to create when I am spending, or at last billing for, 40 hours each week at my day job.

Having not experienced writer's block (yet), it is not a lack of ideas that places this project lower on my list of priorities. Indeed, the class session that was most boring for me identified techniques for developing subjects to write about. With decades of life experience to draw from, I already have more than enough themes and plots to last my next 60 years.

So I have plenty of ideas, but not the motivation to finish my novel, because revising it represents hard work and, like homework assignments in the last term of law school, I can concoct many reasons for not getting to it. Here are recent observations that have turned into handy excuses: the weather is too nice to stay indoors; I could use the next few hours to read T.C. Boyle's latest book; I really should call my mother; revising that court brief one more time is absolutely imperative; that Meryl Streep movie that received wonderful reviews will be leaving the Cineplex soon; I should spend more time with my ever-increasing number of grandchildren; and, this would be an excellent time to experiment with that recipe for *palacsintas*, Hungarian crepes.

Time is passing for me, of course, much faster than it is for writers born after 1948. Which brings me to the elephant in the word processing room: my age and my future as a writer.

Every May or June I read about a nonagenarian who graduates college with her granddaughter. As mentioned, I myself obtained a creative writing degree in the shadow of my seventh decade. I know that Johannes Brahms was 43 when he composed his first symphony at a time when many composers could not make it to the ripe age of 35, that Grandma Moses began painting only after she had reached her 70s, and that the science fiction grandmaster Jack Williamson knocked out his last novel two years before he died at the age of 98. Retirement age, therefore, need not be a deadline or a death sentence for artists.

I keep those facts in perspective as I sporadically peck out what I hope will be my first published novel. But on the other hand, I cannot fool myself: it is likely to be my last, as well.

I simply may not have a second chance to insert my observations and philosophies of a lifetime into a subsequent book. Realistically, this is no time to embark on a seven-part series of novels. So I am forced to make my present draft complete, enfolding everything into this work. That means I should continuously add to my manuscript, delaying the final draft, forcing me to devise even more excuses for its lack of completion.

The result, however, will fall far short of the longest novel ever written. I realize I will never leave a portfolio of published works that rivals the prolific Joyce Carol Oates. I am fully at ease with relinquishing that honor. All I can hope for, then, is recognition for work having more than a modicum of quality.

Someday people may compare Mark Levy's life's work to... oh... William Shakespeare's. "It's just as good," I can hear them say, "and mercifully shorter!"

What's a Patient to Do?

One of my doctors gave me a new list of foods to avoid. This most recent list was a result of an obnoxious kidney stone that, after a month, finally exited down-stage. As much as I am dying to do it, I will refrain from presenting the blow-by-blow events leading up to my stone and me going our separate ways.

I'd like to talk about the list of foods itself. See, I used to think certain items on the list are not toxic; in fact, they are even healthy. I now know better.

Take blueberries, for example. Loaded with antioxidants, right? Wards off cancer better than radiation and chemotherapy, combined. Improves memory. Protects my heart. The more I eat, the healthier I am, correct? Everyone from my doctor to my barber told me so. I had some every morning with my oatmeal when I wanted to feel especially noble; or with my frosted mini donuts when I wanted to neutralize the sugar in what I sometimes call toroidal carbohydrate modules.

But guess what is listed on my *verboten* list because it creates calcium oxalate which, in turn, makes kidney stones faster than you can say, "precipitate?" Yes, it's the innocuous, itty-bitty blueberry, friend of oncologists everywhere.

I'm in a quandary now. Do I continue to have the blueberries for the sake of avoiding cancer but at the risk of kidney stones? Cancer or kidney stones, that's my choice.

After my recent bout with my late, lamented kidney stone, whom I referred to as Rocky, I'm leaning towards cancer as the less painful alternative.

Also on the list of things to avoid if I want to avoid another kidney stone are strawberries, for goodness sake.

I could drink green tea to make up for the loss of berries, since it also is loaded with antioxidants. But the caffeine can lead to a gout attack. So can sardines, hot dogs, wine, and, for my father, turkey.

Then there's cholesterol. If I drink tea, I reduce cholesterol again at the risk of another gout attack.

Garlic, onions, and chili peppers may help prevent cancer, lower cholesterol, or fight fungus, but I've noticed that my friends stand much farther away from me when I'm talking to them, after I've eaten Mexican food.

Some people, like me, take Lipitor to reduce their cholesterol. It turns out, though, that while on Lipitor, I shouldn't eat grapefruit — that wonderful fruit that also helps reduce cholesterol, as well as helps promote weight loss. The combination of grapefruit and Lipitor can result in serious muscle problems. So I can take one or the other, but not both.

Tuna fish is considered a healthy alternative to roast beef and fried chicken, but I have to beware of mercury that can affect my peripheral vision. And that's the least of my problems. It's also been linked to mental illness, and I certainly don't need more of that. Mercurialism can also affect my kidneys, and not in a good way.

Avocados are known to help control diabetes, yet paradoxically, they are loaded with fat.

Bananas are good for potassium, but also carry a large amount of carbs. So do beets and rice and honey and watermelon. The list goes on. It even includes cherries, which are reputed to slow the aging process and protect my heart.

The only things that seem to have no side effects are mushrooms. But with my luck, I'll be poisoned to death on the way to maintaining my health.

Beans are healthful, but come with a risk of gas, as does cabbage.

And speaking of flatulence, certain foods are laxatives, which may not always be advantageous. For example, prunes, of course, are known laxatives, but so are carrots and wheat germ.

All of which brings me back to my donuts. They've got trans fats — whatever that is — white flower, and sugar. They provide too many carbs in the form of sugar, too much unhealthy fat, and the only fiber you'll find is in the bag they come in. In fact, after many years of searching, I have yet to find a single diet that encourages or even allows donuts. But my search continues. There must be something they help except starvation and boredom at meetings. I'm willing to volunteer to help prove a diet high in donuts has a beneficial effect on, say, pellagra or leprosy.

C'mon, *Dunkin' Donuts* — help me out here.

Winning at O.T.B.

The other day I got to the O.T.B. window too late to bet. O.T.B. stands for "Off Track Betting," to those few of you who don't know. With O.T.B., you don't have to actually go to a horse race, braving the weather and the traffic, to lose your money. You can do it from the convenience of a local store front.

And if you're particularly busy or lazy, you can access O.T.B. Internet sites. You can bet online even in your pajamas. There are other advantages, I think, to betting online: there are no people around you to gloat when they win and you don't; and, in the unlikely event that you actually do win a bet, you don't have to worry about a stalker following you into the parking lot to mug you. So betting online takes a lot of pressure off you, the bettor.

Here's another advantage of the O.T.B. experience, instead of attending an actual, physical horse race: you don't have to confine your activities to any particular race track. You can lose your money at a number of tracks almost simultaneously.

Anyway, on that particular day, I approached the O.T.B. cashier. I prefer to call her my discretionary income portfolio manager or DIPM, for short. She is one of three or four DIPMs employed by my local O.T.B. emporium. Sometimes the O.T.B. emporia are called "offices" or "parlors." They all look pretty much alike, whatever they are called. We semi-professional gamblers call the cashiers' stations "windows," but there's no real glass separating my DIPM from me. Some O.T.B. places use Plexiglas, which is probably more difficult to break through when the urge overcomes a disgruntled bettor to throttle his DIPM. In my O.T.B. place, only air separates my agent from my money.

I handed her my betting slip and $2, and she said in a truly apologetic voice, "Sorry, closed out. That race has started."

Now a normal person might be disappointed by that news. After all, I'd spent a fair amount of time deciding which horse to bet my hard-earned wages on. I analyzed the horse's racing history, the jockey's record, the other horses racing against mine, the weather at the race track, and the condition of the track. I even considered the horse's name, but that's a discussion for another day. Mostly, though, I calculated how much money I would win when my selected horse came in. You would think all of that cogitation would have made me angry that I missed the opportunity to bet on the horse of my dreams. Actually, though, I had ambivalent feelings when I was closed out.

You see, I play long shots. In fact, Kate, a good friend of mine, calls me Longshot Levy, an appropriate alliteration under the circumstances. I call her Conservative Kate, to get even. But here's my philosophy: why go through all the work in choosing and betting on a horse that, even if it wins, will pay only a measly dollar on a $2 bet? Doesn't it make sense to bet on a horse that will pay oh, say, $80? You bet it does! State lottery gaming commissions discovered this a long time ago. They decided not to run lottery sweepstakes (Lotto) of five bucks on a $1 bet. And a wise choice it was, in my opinion.

So I usually bet on long shots. To tell the truth, I hardly ever win. Okay, the real truth? I never win.

So when my DIPM informed me that the race had already started, I returned to my seat in front of the eight large TV screens to watch the race with mild interest. I saw the horse I would have bet on take the lead for a few yards, as my picks always do, and then proceed to lose the race.

130

I can hardly describe what a great feeling I had as it came in eighth! For me, it was almost as euphoric a feeling as if I had actually won a long shot. Of course, I could only imagine what that would feel like.

Look how much money I saved by not betting on a losing horse! So now I'm thinking that if my goal at O.T.B. is to walk out of the place happy, I have a great chance of "winning" every time I miss the opportunity to bet. And the more I would have bet, the better I would feel. Imagine not losing $10 or possibly $1,000. There's really no limit to how good I could feel. With meticulous planning, my odds would easily be at least 1 to 100 that I would "win" every time. With odds like that, how can I lose?

I propose changing the name of my sport to Off Track Non-Betting, O.T.N.B. Of course I still have to spend some time deciding which horse not to bet on. A lucky break... well, a lucky break could absolutely ruin my day.

Wish List for Genetic Engineers

In general, I believe the things that futurists predict, although they've been known to make mistakes, like the learned guy who predicted automobiles shouldn't travel faster than 30 mph because the human body would be fatally injured, or the guy at the turn of the last century who thought the 20th century would be the century of the trolley, even though the last trolley car was made in 1924.

But now, futurists are telling us that the 21st century will be the century of biotechnology and I have no reason to disbelieve them. After all, they were right about radio wristwatches, weren't they?

But I'm concerned that scientists may not have clear directions about where we want to go. I mean, left to their own devices, you can't always trust scientists to make right decisions. Take TANG, for instance. How crazy was *that* one?

Here's what I propose: we start a contest to list bio-engineered items we'd like to see in the next hundred years. Just imagine. The sky's the limit. You can propose any biology-based product or improvement you can think of and the bio engineers will figure out how to create it.

I'll start things rolling, to warm you up to this project. Feel free to bombard Robert Conrad with your suggestions. I'm sure he'll look forward to each and every one of them. He may even send you a valuable token of his appreciation, and I'm not talking about a cheap CD or a T-shirt, either.

What I'd love to see in my supermarket are cube-shaped watermelons. That would make cutting watermelons much easier and safer and they'd store in my refrigerator more efficiently, too. What's the big deal? We already have seedless watermelons. It must be a small step, I'm thinking, to go from that marvelous invention to cubical shapes. The hard part is behind us. Hey, doesn't cheese come in rectangular packages? Why can't watermelons? And once we've solved the watermelon problem, we can move on to honeydews, casabas, and eggplants.

While you're at it, scientists, how about adding barcodes directly to the outside skins of watermelons and other growing things? We routinely throw out orange skins and banana skins and, yes, watermelon rinds. What a time saver it would be not to use itty-bitty barcode stickers in the fruit and vegetable section of our supermarkets.

Second suggestion: I'd like to see chickens with more than two wings, since so many of us are fond of Buffalo chicken wings. Seems like a waste of good chickens just to harvest a couple of wings apiece. Why not make chickens with four or six or even seven wings? I think you'll have to agree that's more logical than the present natural variety.

Moving on, but staying with consumable birds, some of us — just admit it — fight over turkey drumsticks on Thanksgiving Day. It should be easy to modify your average breast-enhanced turkey to grow, say, five drumsticks instead of two. That's three more happy people around every Thanksgiving table, the way I figure it.

And speaking of extra legs, why not produce us humans with three legs? We'd be more stable — physically, at least — and the shoe industry could expand by 50%. Everyone wins. Start working on that one, you biotech nerds. And if you have extra time, you might consider adding a third eye to the back of our heads. That would cut down on neck injuries, I'll bet.

133

While you're at it, why not improve humans' eyesight, hearing, and memory, especially as they get older? And speaking of age, how about treating old age like a disease and simply cure it?

So you see how easy it is to give our bio engineers worthwhile goals? They may be smart dudes, but everyone could use a bit of imagination, now and then.

III

COMING AND GOING

Automatic Auto Feature

The automobile, you may recall, was popularized by Henry Ford, who introduced the Model T in 1908, and mass produced it in 1914. But an early version of the automobile engine was patented by Karl Benz in 1879 and Mr. Benz started production of his "motorwagen" in 1888, the year that his wife, Bertha, took a road trip to publicize it.

It wasn't long before certain automatic features were introduced to automobiles. In no particular order, they included the automatic electric starter, the automatic transmission, the automatic AM/FM/satellite-Internet radio, the automatic headlight, the automatic proximity detector, the automatic audible seatbelt reminder, the automatic seat warmer, the automatic wake-up alarm, the automatic engine starter, the automatic audible fuel level reminder, the automatic cell phone answerer, the automatic lane-changing detector, the automatic defroster, the automatic speed control, the automatic blinker-on-too-long reminder, the automatic windshield wiper, the automatic variable windshield wiper, and the automatic rain sensing variable windshield wiper.

So it's not surprising that someone who has followed these technical developments through the patent literature — someone like a handsome patent attorney, for example — might think of yet another automatic auto feature.

Why just last week I happened to be motoring down a local street when a buffoon sped through a stop sign and pulled into traffic, immediately in front of unassuming me. After cursing mildly, as we polite drivers occasionally do, I reached for my horn and honked him loudly, basically to teach him a lesson.

It was then that I thought, "surely, we won't be doing this a hundred years from now." Just like, in a hundred years, we won't have to wait so long to receive our fast food drive-in orders at the end of a long line of cars. And we won't have to be reminded by a flight attendant, or whatever they will be called in a hundred years, how to use a seatbelt on an airplane flight. Oops, bad example. We're doomed to hear seatbelt instructions for a million years.

The point is, we will definitely *not* have to reach for a button to blow our horn at a driver who clearly deserves it. And why is that? Because horn blowing will be automatic in the future! I expect there will be some sort of sensor thing that will detect stupid driving behavior in front of us and will automatically blow our horn at the offending driver.

Just think about that the next time you feel like expressing yourself to some inconsiderate driver who shares the road with you.

Meanwhile, I am starting to work on my automatic cursing feature that will have settings for mild, strong, and blistering.

Can I Get There From Here?

Someone asked Daniel Boone, the 18th Century pioneer and frontiersman, if he ever got lost. "Nope," he allegedly replied, "I never did get lost; but once, for three or four days, I was a might befuddled."

Before I acquired a GPS device, I used to get befuddled quite a bit.

I remember trying to find a specific restaurant in an unfamiliar town. Luckily, a police car was nearby so I could ask for directions.

"How can I get to *The Bloated Mallard* Restaurant?" I asked.

"That's easy," the cop said. "Go a mile and a half down this road. Take a left at *Dunkin' Donuts*. Go about four blocks. Take a right at *Krispy Kreme*. Then down about a mile. Take a right at *Poppy's Original Famous Donuts*. Go two blocks down to *Dunkin' Donuts*."

"Another *Dunkin' Donuts*?" I asked.

"Yup. We have nine Dunkins in this town and I know all of 'em."

The cop was justifiably proud of that factoid.

"Anyway," he continued, "*The Bloated Mallard* is across the street. Can't miss it."

Thank goodness for landmarks, I thought. If it weren't for donut shops, no one would find *The Bloated Mallard* or maybe hundreds of other restaurants nestled among myriad toroidal carbohydrate module establishments in America.

This phenomenon of people relying on landmarks that have special significance to them is not limited to cops and donut shops. One of my inventor clients worked in the gasoline distribution industry. Following directions to his shop, I had to drive past a Shell service station, followed by an Exxon-Mobil, then a Sunoco, and finally a Hess station.

And people who imbibe to excess are known to refer to bars, nightclubs, and liquor stores for directions, day or night. The only occasional problem is the slurred speech of some people eager to help.

A person once directed me to turn where K-mart used to be, but it had been demolished, I eventually learned, five years earlier. If I had been in the town for the last five years, would I have needed the directions in the first place?

Take drive-in movie theaters. They aren't as common as they used to be. In fact, the U.S. has only 356 working drive-in theaters today. That's about seven drive-ins per state, only an eighth the number of theaters we had 50 years ago. So I'm thinking outdoor projector repairmen who want to use drive-ins as landmarks are totally out of luck.

Fast food restaurants outnumber health clubs or fitness centers lately, which is just fine with me. It's as it should be now that we've become the land of the obese. Big, tall, plus size, and full figured people like us get as much exercise maneuvering around dessert buffets as physically fit folks who enjoy working out with instruments of torture.

Heaven knows, clergymen probably use places of worship to locate other places of worship, too. Saint This, Saint That for Catholics; Beth This, Beth That for Jews.

I suppose undertakers can use both funeral parlors and cemeteries as landmarks to direct their clientele. That must be some small comfort to the bereaved.

Discrimination in the Air

One of the great pleasures of flying on a commercial airplane in the United States nowadays is removing your smelly, tight-fitting shoes and placing them on a conveyor belt so the TSA screener can be sure you don't try to blow up the plane. The second half of the process requires you to put your shoes back on and — in my case, at least — retying your shoelaces while the person traveling with you acts as if your delay really isn't bothering her in the least.

Now, I enjoy the routine as much as anyone. But as I was struggling to squeeze my right foot into my left shoe on my last trip, I began to reflect on a couple of ideas. First, why don't I buy a pair of slip-on shoes for air travel? And second, what is the reason for continuing to participate in what seems like this pointless, remove-your-shoes exercise?

As you recall, a very long time ago — actually, more than a decade ago — a terrorist named Richard Reid thought he could make a statement by packing C-4 plastic explosives in his sneakers and igniting them from his seat on a Boeing 767. He didn't get too far.

A flight attendant and other passengers noticed his behavior and subdued him. He was removed from the plane, tried, convicted, and sentenced to life in prison at a supermax facility in Colorado.

That arch criminal soon became known, far and wide, as the "shoe bomber," which, I think, is a reward totally out of proportion to his activities. If he actually ignited his shoe bomb, maybe I could see him earning that title. But he was unsuccessful, yet he's still known as the shoe bomber. It's just flat unfair. I mean, I'm usually unsuccessful at lighting my barbecue grill, but nobody calls me the "barbecue starter," do they?

Thanks to the shoe bomber, we all have to take both our shoes off every time we visit our grandchildren.

Actually, that's not quite the case. I recently learned that passengers at at least one airport don't have to remove their shoes if they are more than 75 years old. Another airport states that children 12 and younger are exempt. Terrorists haven't necessarily instilled terror into our lives, but they have made our lives more confusing. Apparently, the TSA has discovered the chance of a pre-teenager or a senior citizen packing C-4 plastic explosives in his shoes is about zero.

Who determined that a 74 ½ year old represents a greater shoe bombing risk than a 75 year old? This arbitrary age limit strikes me as blatant age discrimination, especially since, as far as I know, the TSA has never detected another pair of shoes with explosives in them, regardless of the owner's age.

If I weren't so close to the magic age myself, I would rally my fellow shoeless travelers at the airport. At the risk of stubbing our toes, we would march down Concourse B, right past the overpriced Starbucks kiosk, and we would protest this practice.

Drinking and Driving

Our country has had a love/hate relationship with alcohol for a long time. Remember the Prohibition Act that became the 18th Amendment to the Constitution? That passed in 1919 and prohibited manufacture, sale, or transportation of intoxicating liquors in the United States. It took another Amendment, the 21st, to repeal it when Congress finally sobered up almost 15 years later. The 18th Amendment was the only one to be repealed in its entirety. Wow, 15 years of Prohibition! Just the thought of it is enough to drive me to drink.

Speaking of which, when we focus on drinking and driving, it's only natural that we try to stamp out the drinking part. It's a proud part of our national genetics, apparently. Under federal and state laws, a person under the age of 21 cannot consume or even purchase alcohol, period. And it doesn't matter whether he drives or even whether he has a driver's license. I think that's driving too far in the wrong direction. If we're concerned about drunk drivers, it seems to me we ought to go after drunks who are likely to drive, not go after every 20-year-old even if he has no problem walking a straight line.

Here's the other side of the issue. As much as we've demonized alcohol, we've also glorified automobiles. I can understand that. Ever since they were invented, cars have represented freedom and independence. And we are nothing if not a nation of freedom lovers. Do you want to get away from your parents? Hey, drive a car. Do you want to get away from that boring job? Well, drive off for a vacation. Do you want to avoid paying child support? Fine. Drive to another state.

Nowadays, I think young drivers are influenced by video games. The penalty for losing a video game is not bodily injury; it's merely having to hit the RESTART button and play the game again. In the old days — well, like the 1980s — a player who visited a video arcade might run his cartoon car off his animated road and lose a quarter. Painful, but not fatal. Of course now every kid has video games on his computer or PDA or electronic whatnot, so there's a great incentive for young players to take chances. That makes for uninhibited and aggressive drivers. When translated into real automobiles, unfortunately, even the Jaws of Life may not be able to save the young victims.

When I see some crazy driver on the road, zigging and zagging, endangering the lives of innocent people like me, it's usually *not* a drunk person, but it's almost always a young person. As a formerly young person myself, as reckless as the next young driver, I have to admit, I must point out the obvious: dangerous drivers are not always inebriated, but they're often young. Insurance companies know this, so they charge higher premiums for young drivers. But that hardly slows the kids down.

Yet the driving age continues to decrease. In North Dakota, for example, a child as young as 14 1/2 can get a driver's license, which is actually six months older than a kid in Kansas. On farms in certain states, trucks can be operated by even younger drivers.

When a kid is that young, he or she can be easily distracted. Music, conversation or girls in bikinis are popular culprits. It's not only young ones who can lose concentration, though. Last year I smacked right into a street sign while engrossed on my cell phone. Here's the embarrassing thing: at the time, I was walking on the sidewalk. The street sign, you'll be relieved to know, was unscathed.

We'd have fewer accidents — fatal or otherwise — if we had a high national driving age, like we have for drinking. How about an older driving age of, say, 35? If a person has to be at least 35 to be elected President, why not also make it the lowest age to operate an instrument of death?

After all, it can take years of experience to learn how to hold one's liquor.

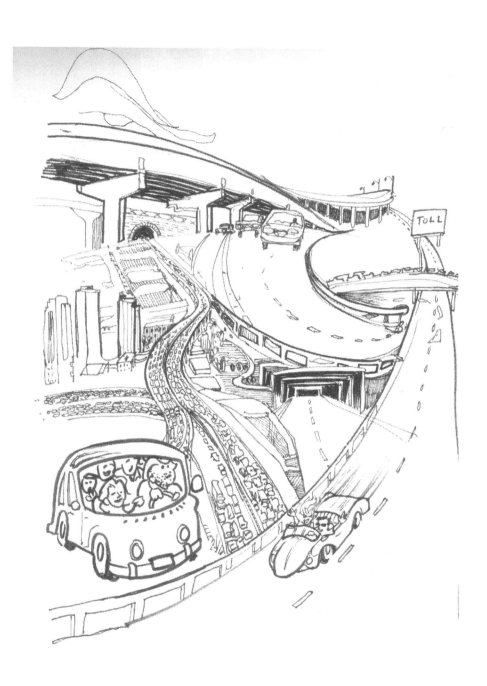

Express Lanes

Now that I live in south Florida, I spend a fair amount of time in my car on Interstate 95, which is a multi-lane highway running north and south and passing through downtown Miami. At rush hour, or when we're inconvenienced by construction or motor vehicle crashes or a hurricane, this 12-lane road can host miles of bumper-to-bumper traffic.

The folks in charge of roadways — they're probably called vehicular flow control analytic engineers, or something equally obscure and impressive — these folks came up with an interesting partial solution to the traffic problem on I-95: they introduced express lanes. And Miami isn't alone. Since the 1990s, other highways connecting large cities have toll road bypass or express lanes, too.

The concept of express lanes is based on the assumption that certain people are more important than the rest of us, so their time is naturally more valuable than ours.

The vehicle flow engineers take advantage of the fact that many of these extremely important people have more discretionary income than your everyday worker ant who commutes in a beat-up, old, Ford pickup. On parts of I-95, in fact, sometimes you can't throw a rock without hitting a Ferrari or a Lamborghini.

The highway planners decided to give these rich SOBs — I mean VIPs — an option to speed up their commute. For a fee, they can enter a seven-mile stretch of road isolated from the rest of the highway and separated by barriers, so they can't change their mind once they're on this special road. It's called an express lane and, at least in theory, it allows the driver to bypass slower traffic. I say, "in theory," because sometimes a crash — we don't say "accidents" anymore — sometimes a crash occurs on an express lane and traffic slows down or comes to a dead stop. So now you have a lane or two of outrageously expensive vehicles at a standstill, trapped in the express lane. I wonder if the irony is lost on those VIPs, while sitting in their overheating cars, watching hundreds of pickup trucks whiz by them. I know it strikes me as particularly piquant, as I cruise into town, hell bent for leather.

Of course, rich people aren't the only ones who may use express lanes. We live in a democracy, after all, so every person — even the least significant of us — has the right to fritter away his money as he sees fit. Let's say you have some money left over after paying for car maintenance, inspections (if you don't live in Florida), E-Z passes or Sun passes (if you do live in Florida), insurance premiums, and parking; and after buying gasoline, tires, and — now that I think of it — buying or leasing your vehicle in the first place. Do you want to spend your remaining cash on an express lane? It's a question I ask myself on the rare occasion I'm on that road and I have money not earmarked for luxury items or for the veterinarian's bills.

The express lane program uses value pricing. The experience costs you more when traffic is congested. That's understandable. If you're going to save 30 minutes on your commute, shouldn't you expect to pay more than if you're going to save only 3 minutes? A big, electronic road sign lets you know how much the express lane experience will cost you at that time.

Frankly, I myself have been tempted to speed up my journey on occasion. But here's my dilemma: thanks to value pricing, I can enter an express lane during off rush hour times for only 25¢. The traffic — what there is of it — is moving smoothly, so it seems foolish to pay even a quarter to be in an express lane that won't save me time.

On the other hand, when traffic is backed up, the I-95 "highwaymen" (I'll call them) charge $4.75 for the privilege of bypassing the bumper-to-bumper suckers. Unless I'm rushing to cash in a winning lottery ticket, say, that fee seems excessive. For that much money, I could be sipping a Starbucks Java Chip Mocha Light Frappuccino Grande in my car as I inch down the highway in the slow lane with fellow travelers.

So it comes down to this: if the express lane fee is too low, it's obviously not worth bypassing non-existent traffic; and if it's too high, I can't afford it. Either way, I'll leave the express lane option to the Bentley and Maserati folks who don't have time to listen to this essay, anyway.

Find a Grave

Quick: Who is buried in Grant's Tomb? You know, the one at Riverside Drive and West 122nd Street in Manhattan. Grant's Tomb, by the way, is formally called the General Grant National Memorial. Of course, Ulysses S. Grant is buried there, but so is Julia Boggs Grant, the first lady of that 18th president. Turns out she was four years younger than Grant, and died in 1902, 17 years after he did.

Ulysses' buddies at West Point gave him the nickname, "Sam," which he carried until he died.

But back to Julia. She attended the Misses Mauros boarding school in St. Louis which catered to daughters of affluent parents. Her oldest brother was a friend of Sam Grant from his days at West Point.

Julia's father didn't want her to marry Grant, because he was too poor. But they did get married. Grant's family refused to attend the wedding because of the slaves that Julia's father owned. Throughout the Civil War, Julia Grant accompanied her husband near the site of battles, often staying in his tent.

"Goodness, Mark," I can hear you say. "How did you become such an expert on Julia Grant?"

I just found another website, that's how. It's FindAGrave.com and it has 152 million grave sites along with some detailed history of the graves' inhabitants.

For example, during the First World War, Thomas Edison was 70 years old and the government asked him to serve. He built a factory in 18 days to help the army and navy. He obtained his 1,093rd patent at age 83.

The set of graves on the FindAGrave website isn't limited to presidents and inventors. It includes sports figures, actors, musicians, artists, politicians, criminals, and gangsters. Of course there is some overlap among politicians and criminals, but I'm not here to judge.

Once you find who you are looking for on the website, you can read a short biography and see one or more photos. I noticed Julia Grant is a formidable and handsome woman. You can also learn the deceased's cause of death, if you're interested.

Of course, you can find the precise location of each grave. The website provides you not only with the name of the cemetery, but also with the longitude and latitude, so you can hone in on your favorite hero or anti-hero unless, like Robin Williams, the deceased was cremated and his ashes strewn over the Pacific Ocean.

You can leave a message regarding the deceased on the site and you can read messages left by others.

I found that browsing through the FindAGrave website is almost as much fun as strolling through an old cemetery and you can do it even in rainy weather.

Food is My Destination

It's almost impossible for me to get interested in visiting a foreign country or even a foreign city. When I say "foreign," I mean any location more than 20 miles away from my home in upstate New York. Maybe it's because I like my house so much. Or more likely, it's because I don't particularly like to travel. For me, walking to my mailbox is a trip.

Sure, I have a fear of flying, like most human beings with an IQ greater than 65, but I also dislike buses, boats, trains, trucks and cars. I'm not especially fond of ski mobiles, either, or jet skis, water skis, motorcycles or parachutes. There's something about being rooted to the ground that I find hard to beat.

So in order to undertake a journey, I have to be assured that the destination is worth the trip. It takes a lot of motivation to separate me from my home. If I have to pack and then unpack, and figure out how to outsmart the electronic ticket machine at the airport, and take off my shoes and my belt, and empty my pockets, and unload my camera and dismantle my laptop computer, and discard my toothpaste tube, and wedge my carry-on luggage into that tiny, overhead compartment, and squeeze into an airplane seat in the middle of the row, between two NFL linemen, and run from the far end of a terminal to a connecting flight miles away, and hang out at the baggage delivery carousel until all of the other bags from three flights have been delivered, well, I'm not going to do all that merely to see some museum or bridge or large hole in the ground.

No, it's going to take a lot more than some wonder of the

world to get me to board a plane, nowadays. It's going to take... food! And not just any food I can buy locally at, say, McDonald's or Wal-Mart. It's going to take some exotic treat that I can get only at my destination. Like hot, crusty sourdough bread in San Francisco, or a sumptuous barbeque pork sandwich in Houston, or spicy bouillabaisse in New Orleans, or succulent crab cakes in Baltimore, or reindeer jerky in Fairbanks, Alaska.

Speaking of which, I'm a bit wary of absolutely new foods. No, it's not because I'm squeamish, but because I fear I may simply LOVE the item and it may be next to impossible to taste it again, except in the unlikely event that I return to that faraway place. I mean, where can I possibly get reindeer jerky in the lower 48 states?

The Internet, of course, is a great leveler. Online, I can order anything I've ever heard of — and a number of things I haven't. But have you seen the prices they're charging for reindeer jerky lately? I have to think twice before mail ordering 20 pounds of the stuff.

I've had some very tasty items in faraway places. Like Cincinnati chili — they serve it on spaghetti, you know — and Philadelphia cheese steak — nothing like the stuff most of us might buy in our supermarket frozen food section, and Atlantic City salt water taffy and Wisconsin cheddar, and Vermont maple syrup — not the diluted stuff — and New York cheesecake.

When I was forced to travel to Minneapolis recently, I went to a fair that offered deep fried Twinkies and deep fried Oreo cookies, if you can believe that. Frankly, I thought that destination wasn't worth removing my shoes for.

Geographic Dishes

Although I recorded this piece in a state-of-the-art recording studio at WSKG, my fine local radio station in Binghamton, I actually wrote it months earlier beside a waterfall at a remote jungle in Ecuador. My choice was to take along a writing pad or bug spray and —SLAP— the bug spray didn't make it. The waterfall was noisy, so you might want to run your shower at full blast for the next three minutes to recreate the appropriate atmosphere.

Here's an interesting factoid about Ecuador: a specialty or delicacy among the natives — believe it or not — is guinea pig roasted on a skewer. You can Google that, if you like. Try searching Ecuador and guinea pig. You may wish to skip the images if you haven't had breakfast yet.

Becoming a vegan a few weeks ago, I had a good excuse not to indulge in *arroz con cuy* or guinea pig and rice. Besides, I feared that I might like the little critters, and that could be a problem in Binghamton. How could I visit my local pet store twice a week, and claim to be a vegan, you know?

Anyway, it occurred to me that many locations are associated with particular foods or drinks. Take succulent Maine lobster, hearty Idaho potatoes and warm Texas toast, all of which would make a tasty meal that could be washed down with Long Island iced tea. Sharp Vermont cheddar, Buffalo hot wings, and meaty Maryland crabcakes might make tempting appetizers for that meal. If you're still hungry, there's always steaming Virginia ham, or crispy Peking duck for those into the international scene, or a finger-lickin' portion of what used to be called Kentucky Fried Chicken before the "F" word was banned, of course. You could finish off the meal with a sweet, maybe flaming dessert made from Georgia peaches.

When I lived in Colorado, a friend introduced me to Chicago beef. It's shaved prime rib served on a roll with a generous helping of warm steak juice poured over it. It's pretty similar to a Philadelphia cheese steak, minus the cheese. But I had an occasion to visit Chicago recently — this was before I turned vegan — and I discovered the same sandwich on a menu. It wasn't called Chicago beef in Chicago; they called it Italian beef. Speaking of Chicago, there's a long-standing rivalry between Chicago and New York pizza lovers.

But you don't see either city claiming Ecuadorian guinea pig as its own, do you?

Getting Directions

I once heard that a New Yorker will never admit he doesn't know how to get somewhere. So if you are lost in Manhattan and ask someone for directions, you'll always get them, regardless of whether they're accurate.

I haven't lived in New York City for a long time, but when someone in the city asks me how to get somewhere, I always tell them something. I figure that by the time the lost soul realizes that my directions were incorrect, I'll be miles away. And even if I stayed in the exact same spot, what are the odds that the person will come all the way back to confront me? Let's face it: what are the odds the person will even know how to get back to where we had the short conversation?

Of course, this works the other way around, too. When I'm in a strange location and I ask for directions, the chances are pretty good that the person I ask is as clueless as I am. But I give them the benefit of the doubt and follow their instructions, however ridiculous they may seem.

People don't ask directions as much as they used to, thanks to GPS systems and online maps. But I guess I'm an exception, because it seems like I can't find my way out of a paper bag. And either there's a Mapquest conspiracy or I'm becoming dyslexic in my old age, but those online maps don't always make sense.

People giving directions often use landmarks, which can be a good thing, but not when the presumably knowledgeable person assumes that I live in the neighborhood and, in fact that

I've lived there for some time. I can tell that I'm mistaken for a native when the real native says things like, "You know where Fred's grocery store used to be?" or "Go about a mile down this road and turn right where Orville's bait shop was before they tore it down."

I have a friend who's in the auto service station supply business. To him, all landmarks are gas stations. He's pretty good at it, too. He knows where the Sunoco stations are, the Mobile stations, and the Hess stations. Occasionally, a station will change from one brand to another, which can cause problems, as you would guess. Frankly, I didn't know our town *had* so many gas stations until I needed directions from him to get to the east side from the west side.

Police officers are a pretty good bet, when it comes to knowing their way around town. A while ago, I was trying to find an obscure new restaurant in Elmira. The cop I asked was extremely polite and helpful, but I noticed that he used a donut shop as a landmark at every turn.

The directions went something like this: "Go half a mile to the Dunkin' Donuts and make a left turn. Go about 3/4 of a mile and bear left at the Krispy Kreme. Then it's only a half a mile, just past Winchell Donuts on the right."

I just hope I never stop an undertaker for directions by mistake. I'll be taking a tour of funeral homes for half the night.

How I Know I'm Not in Florida

I moved from south Florida to Evergreen, Colorado a few years ago. The other night, a nightmare woke me up. I dreamt I was still in Florida, yet many things were different.

I noticed a big display of snow shovels at the supermarket with a sign that indicated they are on sale year 'round.

This is definitely not Florida, I thought. But I still didn't have a clue as to where I was.

I asked for directions to a Burger King. When I said "Thank you," the helpful person said, "You bet." I lived in Florida for some time, but no one ever said, "You bet."

Things got even stranger when I stopped a rabbi who happened to be strolling down the street in front of the Burger King. I asked where I could get a good bagel with a shmear of cream cheese.

"Hmmm," he said. "You might have to go to Las Vegas."

How did I get to Nevada? I thought. But just then, I noticed a newspaper I recognized. It was printed in Evergreen, Colorado. Now that's about 600 miles from Las Vegas. The Denver airport itself takes an hour to reach from Evergreen. Since a roundtrip airplane ticket to Vegas from Denver goes for $330, without baggage, if I decided to buy a dozen bagels, I'd be paying $27.50 per bagel. I have to tell you, some Sunday mornings it feels like it would be worth it.

So I woke up abruptly at the thought of spending two days and a week's salary for a bagel. But I continued to think about the things that tell me I'm not in Florida anymore.

For instance, it's difficult to find Bermuda shorts and Hawaiian shirts in Colorado department stores for nine months of the year. That's a big difference from the shops along the tourist streets of Miami.

Restaurants don't offer early bird specials here in Colorado. That's unfortunate, because I got used to them on South Beach. And speaking of the beach, there aren't nearly as many bikinis here. In fact, I haven't seen one of them since August.

Elk crossing signs abound in Colorado, a sight I don't remember seeing in Florida. On the other hand, there are precious few alligators in Colorado and, of course, not too many warning signs about them.

I've also seen signs on the I-70 interstate in Colorado advising truckers about steep hills. One of them says, "Trucks, Don't be Fooled — 4 more miles of steep grades and sharp curves." Not much chance of trucks being fooled in Florida, since the highest elevation is Britton Hill, 345 feet. I know what you're thinking: What about Mount Trashmore, the landfill site in northern Broward County, Florida. But that's only 225 feet high and, technically, it doesn't count because it's an artificial mountain.

Buffalo burgers and elk steaks are on many Colorado menus, but the number of Cuban restaurants here is limited and I can't find conch fritters, alligator bites, or mango smoothies at my local barbecue place.

I notice fewer Maseratis and Ferraris around here, especially when we have more than two feet of snow, which is pretty often. The cars here have more ski racks than I remember in Florida.

Sports stores display horse saddles, but nary a surf board. That's probably because there are more horses and rodeos than barrel waves in the lakes here.

The yellow pages of my Evergreen phone book fail to list one of the most entertaining spectator sports in Florida: alligator wrestling.

People here smoke funny-looking cigarettes occasionally, but they're not furtive and they don't look over their shoulders like they do in Florida.

Perhaps the biggest change from Florida to Colorado is I can't see the ocean from here. The Rocky Mountains get in the way. You bet they do.

Let's Not Take a Trip

I've been giving some thought lately as to why people like to travel. That's not easy for me, since I personally detest the experience. I have rarely found that the effort was worth the reward. With the airlines succumbing to every little suggestion proposed by the Transportation Security Administration or TSA, as it likes to be called, traveling has gotten much worse for all of us. Nevertheless, I'm going to try to put myself in the position of at least one of the 700 million travelers who board airplanes every year in the U.S. Now to be fair, a high percentage of those travelers have to travel for their jobs. But it turns out, over half of all international travelers are motivated only by recreation — you know, tours and vacations.

I think it all boils down to this: people who want to go somewhere, especially for recreation, are not going towards a destination so much as running away from their present location. They're simply not happy being home. They'd rather be somewhere else.

When you think about that, so much discontent is pretty sad. These people have settled in one part of the country, in a somewhat hospitable or at least a tolerable climate, found an apartment or a house — or maybe even built one — that they can almost afford in a neighborhood that's close to shopping and schools and houses of worship and jobs and transportation.

At one time, when they first moved into their new home, they provided their new address to the Post Office and the utilities company and the IRS. They told their friends and at least some of their relatives where they moved. They packed up their belongings from their previous place and moved them to their new place. They touched up the new place, giving it a thorough cleaning and perhaps some paint. They may even have added a new bathroom, because we all have a love affair with indoor plumbing and you can never have too many bathrooms, as John or Thomas Crapper could have said.

Anyway, when these people first arrived, they introduced themselves to their new neighbors, made small talk, and tried to find common interests, starting with politics and moving to recommendations for good, local pizza.

That's a fair amount of work, when you think of it, to relocate to the home of their dreams. And just when the dust settled and they could relax in their new abode, they decided to take a trip.

Now they're standing on line at an airport, shoes in one hand and everything else that might tick off the airport gendarmes in the other.

And for what? To take pictures of some exotic animal, some ancient ruins, or some fantastic natural rock formation? Oh, please! Don't tell me they can't get just about any still or moving image they want on the Discovery Channel or on a DVD, complete with natural sounds, music, and instructional narration, for a ridiculously small fraction of the price of an airline ticket.

They can even buy a computer for less money than the price of most airline tickets. With digital photo software, they can insert pictures of themselves in photos that they download from the Internet. Just think of the possibilities if they start with a picture of Mt. Rushmore, for example. And they can see their slides or watch their DVDs over and over, whenever they choose, from the comfort of their very own couch at just the right temperature, and nary a mosquito in sight.

So you see, there's really no reason to travel nowadays. Get with the 21st Century. That's my advice. And stay home. What are we, couch potatoes or Vikings?

Magic Cities

Guess how many states have cities nicknamed, Magic City? I'll get you started. In addition to Miami, Florida, Roanoke, Virginia, and Bogalusa, Louisiana, of course, eleven other cities have Magic City nicknames including Colon, Michigan, which modestly calls itself "The Magic Capital of the World."

So when someone asks you what do Gary, Indiana, Birmingham, Alabama, and Billings, Montana have in common, you can say they're all known as magic cities.

The northernmost Magic City in America is Minot (MY-not), North Dakota. The town was named after Henry D. Minot, an investor in the Great Northern Railway. This is only the first of a number of railroad stories connected with Magic Cities. Within five months of the 1886 founding of Minot, it had grown to 5,000 residents, about the same number of Air Force personnel who now live on the Minot Air Force Base, close to the town. Minot got its nickname from the fact that the original tent city sprang up overnight. The Air Force Base, by the way, is home to some nuclear weapons, but I'm sure that's not why the military personnel call it Why-not. I'm glad the nickname for Minot is the Magic City rather than, say, Kaboom City.

The easternmost Magic City is Millinocket, Maine. In 1898, because of the speed with which Millinocket, Maine grew, it gained the nickname Magic City. Are you seeing a trend here? You ain't seen nothing yet.

The magic city with the highest elevation is Leadville, Colorado at 10,000 feet and the lowest is Miami at six. That may not be high enough to survive the rising ocean level in the next hundred years. Bogalusa is a close second, elevation-wise, at 95 feet. Bogalusa got its nickname in 1906 when it was constructed with several hotels, a number of churches, a YMCA, and a YWCA in less than a year. It is located along a creek called Bogue Lusa, which means Dark Waters.

You wouldn't think Moberly, Missouri would warrant the name, Magic City, since its only claim to fame appears to be the fact that this was the point where two railroads connected with the North Missouri Railroad Company. In fact, it was named after Colonel William E. Moberly, the first president of the Chariton and Randolph County railroads. Explosive growth occurred in 1873, when the town sprang from the prairie overnight, like magic. Hence, the name.

Barberton, Ohio started growing rapidly in 1891, as a planned industrial community so it became known as the Magic City, too. It was named by Akron industrialist, Ohio Columbus Barber, known to his friends as O.C., who had taken over his father's match company that began during the 1860s and '70s. O.C. also named the town's natural lake, Lake Anna, for his daughter. O.C. consolidated a number of similar factories and changed its name to the Diamond Match Company. "Magic Match" would have been a nice, alliterative name, I think, but I wasn't consulted. The company produced 250 million matches a day, leading me to suspect that only a magic spell could prevent the whole town from incinerating eventually.

South Omaha, Nebraska got the Magic City nickname in 1890 due to — what else? — impressive growth, this time thanks to the Union Stockyards.

Roanoke, Virginia, in 1884 became a city so quickly that it earned the nickname Magic City and is the largest municipality in Southwest Virginia.

Billings, Montana was named for Frederick Billings, the railroad baron who was president of the Northern Pacific

Railway. If you'd like to establish a town and name it after yourself, first get yourself elected president of a railroad. The rest is easy. Frederick never actually stayed in Billings overnight. And that's your trivia fact of the day. Oh, almost forgot: its nickname, the Magic City, was developed due to its rapid growth since 1882, etc., etc.

And now we come to Miami, Florida. In 1896 the population was about 1,000. Today, after a bit more than a century, Miami's metro area, which grew to encompass the whole county, is the fourth-largest urban area in the United States, with a population of about five and a half million. Needless to say, the growth from one year to the next was like magic. The city is magic to me because it's home to my Chihuahua, Cashew the Wonder Dog. It's also a nice place to live if you'd rather not deal with snow in your driveway anymore. At least five and a half million people agree.

Gary, Indiana is called Magic City for short, but longer versions include America's Magic Industrial City, the Magic City of Steel, and the City of the Century, because of its rapid growth. Unfortunately, the magic is gone in Gary, the rust belt city with an enormous debt, fewer people, and fewer jobs than ever.

Colon, Michigan has a happier story. It is home to Abbott's Magic Manufacturing Company, the world's largest producer of magic paraphernalia, which was started in 1934 by Percy Abbott and Harry Blackstone, the famous magician and illusionist, who is buried there. In fact, the town cemetery proudly boasts the final resting place for about 30 magicians. Some of them are more famous than others, but they're all dead.

At the annual Magic Get-Together in August, besides coming to die and be buried, magicians from around the world visit the village of Colon to perform, meet fellow performers, and purchase new magic acts and illusions. The Abbott Magic

Company hosts an event in downtown Colon with nightly performances at the Colon High School Auditorium. To some outsiders, the town is known as the Home of Hocus Pocus. You can't throw a magic wand in August without bouncing of a magician or a magician wannabee.

Although the term, Magic City, is now a cliché, it does have a nicer ring than, say, Unforeseen-and-Explosive-Growth-at-the-End-of-the-Nineteenth-Century City.

Many Capitals of the World

Although there is only one grits capital of the world, there are two fruitcake, four strawberry, and five watermelon capitals of the world. Grits is or are Warwick, Georgia's claim to fame, but both Claxton, Georgia and Corsicana, Texas believe they're the fruitcake capital. Strawberries are touted by Oxnard and also Watsonville in California; Ponchatoula, Louisiana; and Chadbourn, North Carolina. Not to be left out, Plant City in Florida is the winter strawberry capital of the world. When it comes to watermelon, the capital of the world may be Cordele, Georgia; Hope, Arkansas; Rush Springs, Oklahoma; or Naples or Weatherford, both in the state of Texas. But it's Thomson, Illinois that may trump them all as, simply, the melon capital.

Horseradish? Collinsville, Illinois; Eau Claire, Wisconsin; and Tulelake, California have to fight that one out, maybe over slabs of prime rib.

When it comes to fish, a catfight is brewing over the catfish capital, among Demopolis, Alabama; Belzoni, Mississippi; and Des Allemands, Louisiana.

The speckled perch capital is Okeechobee, Florida, which, if you ask my opinion, should also be the whimsical town name capital. Just try to say Okeechobee without smiling.

Geneva, New York is the lake trout capital, whereas Gleason, Wisconsin is the brook trout fishing capital. Breaux Bridge, Louisiana is the crayfish — or crawfish if you live there — capital. And speaking of regional pronunciations, Madison, Minnesota is the lutefisk — or lutfisk if you live there — capital. Rockland, Maine is the lobster capital, yet Crisfield, Maryland and

Calabash, North Carolina are clawing each other to be the seafood capital.

Although Fernandina Beach, Florida isn't the shark capital, it claims to be the shark's tooth capital of the world, but it has to share that honor with another city in Florida: Venice.

Oakdale, California or perhaps Bandera, Texas may be the cowboy capital of the world, but it's Wickenburg, Arizona that is the dude ranch capital. Cody, Wyoming is the rodeo capital. And if any of those cowboys feel like having dinner, they might want to go to Lincoln, Nebraska, the steak capital of the world.

Veggies are popular items for towns to argue about. For example, Stockton and Isleton, both in California and Hadley, Massachusetts all expect people to think of them when they pour hollandaise sauce over their asparagus.

It's fun to see the fruits, events, and contraptions that certain cities and towns claim as their own. For example, Eau Claire, Michigan is the cherry pit spitting capital of the world, even though Traverse City, also in Michigan, and Linden, California both claim to be the actual cherry capital.

Albertville, Alabama is the fire hydrant capital of the world. Apparently, no other community reveres them quite as much. The bicycle capital is Davis, California. Pearsonville, California is the hubcap capital of the world. You'd think it would also be the pothole capital, but neither Pearsonville nor any other town wants to claim that distinction.

Scottsboro, Alabama is known as the lost luggage capital of the world. And speaking of lost items, Fort Payne, Alabama happens to be the sock capital of the world. Some of my lost socks may be waiting for me there.

Green Bay, Wisconsin is the toilet paper capital. The crutch capital is Rumney, New Hampshire. And Windom, Kansas is the covered dish capital.

It's just logical that Vidalia, Georgia is the sweet onion capital while Hershey, Pennsylvania is the chocolate capital. And where but Battle Creek, Michigan would the breakfast capital of the world be located?

Seattle, Washington is the coffee capital. No surprise there. Douglas, Wyoming is the jackalope capital, and I can't say I'm surprised about that one, either.

Some town in Idaho must claim to be the potato capital of the world, don't you think? It's Blackfoot, Idaho.

Washington, Missouri is the corn cob pipe capital. The underwear capital is Knoxville, Tennessee. Anchor-age, Alaska is the hanging basket capital. Strong, Maine claims to be the toothpick capital and earmuffs are featured in Farmington, Maine.

Rosewell, New Mexico is — what else? — the alien capital of the world, not to be confused with Elmwood, Wisconsin, which is the UFO capital, or Willow Creek, California, the bigfoot capital.

Anthony, New Mexico and Anthony, Texas are the leap year capitals of the world, whatever that means.

Binghamton, New York has six of the 150 working antique carousels in North America, making it the carousel capital of the world.

Owensboro, Kentucky is the barbecued mutton capital. Westfield, New York is the grape juice capital presumably for washing down all that mutton.

In the "watch where you step" category, Beaver, Oklahoma is the cow chip capital. The wild goose capital is Sumner, Missouri. And Rayne, Louisiana is the frog capital. The firefly capital is Boone, North Carolina.

In Pennsylvania, Punxsutawney is the weather capital, despite the fact that the groundhog capital is Sun Prairie, Wisconsin.

New York City and the District of Columbia understandably both claim to be *The* capital of the world, but Cosmopolis, Washington squeezes in as the city of the world.

This little informative piece should help you plan your next trip, especially if you are a strawberry-eating, cherry-pit-spitting, lost-luggage-seeking, leap-year-traveling, shark tooth collector.

Moving Day

The average family in America — you know, father, mother and 1.8 children — accumulates 700 pounds of stuff every year. I got this statistic from a moving man a few years ago — and I have no reason to doubt it — as he helped transport my family's things into his moving van.

While he was struggling with the legs of our baby grand piano, I calculated that we now had 14,000 more pounds than we had when we moved into the house 20 years ago. Seven tons. That's a lot of kitchen devices, books, photographs, and knick-knacks.

I should have learned from my experiences, moving the contents of my house half a dozen times, but the fact is, I didn't give it a second thought when I decided to move my office earlier in the year. I hired a moving company. What could be simpler? It wasn't I, but the moving company that would have to deal with office furniture and machines that make my life easier — like fax machines, copiers, computers, toaster ovens, microwaves, and electric pencil sharpeners. And it wasn't I, but the moving company that would handle the many paper files accumulated over years and, of course, the heavy file cabinets they were stored in.

Seven hundred pounds per year? I only wish.

The packers provided the flattened boxes and they kept on coming, like a dry version of the Sorcerer's Apprentice.

"Oh, we'll never need all of these boxes," I declared.

But of course we did. Over 120 boxes, transported as efficiently as overgrown bricks down an assembly line, and weighing just about as much. Paper is heavy, as we all know. A ream of 20 lb. copier paper weighs 5 pounds. Each of my boxes filled with paper weighed about 35 pounds. A hundred twenty boxes? Over two tons.

So far, so good. I didn't have to get my hands dirty on this first phase of the project, since the moving men and women — bless them — did all the packing and heavy lifting. It was the next day, when those 120 boxes arrived at my new office, that the fun began. It wasn't the moving company, but I who had to find a place for every precious sheet of paper.

Office business didn't stop or even slow down merely because the office had been moved. The phone continued to ring and the mail continued to pile up. The email... well, don't get me started. When I had to find a file, it was inevitably located in a box surrounded by, and buried under, a stack of other boxes. Everything I wanted to do required at least three earlier actions or conditions precedent, as we say in the legal biz.

It's been over a month now since I moved, but I'm still unloading boxes. They're everywhere. I can't walk a straight line from any part of a room to any other without skirting around a box or two. It's a logistical obstacle course.

Lately, I've been having nightmares about boxes tumbling from the sky and landing heavily, one atop another on my desk, like a dark, suffocating Tetris game. And if I don't wake up in time, the next part of the dream is when all of the boxes burst open and my erstwhile, well-organized files whip up into a blizzard, a tornado of paper.

From now on, I resolve to migrate my business to a paperless system. I'll start by writing these essays on my arm.

Popular Google Searches by State

You can learn a lot about people from the questions they ask. I was interested to see the topics people from different states investigate using Google. An online real estate web site called Estately.com collected data by running search queries for words, terms, and questions through Google Trends. What they found was both surprising and not so surprising.

Take Texas, for example. Texas residents google the question, "Do I have herpes?" more than residents in any other state. Texans also want to know if dinosaurs are real, are zombies real, and does beer make you fat. You wouldn't think you need Google to answer any of those questions, and a quick trip to your local health clinic should clear up the herpes question, if not herpes itself.

Utah residents have questions about the Church of Jesus Christ of Latter-day Saints. No surprise there. They also want to know whether global warming is a hoax and they like to know all about Twinkies.

Wisconsin residents are obsessed with Beanie Babies and survival shelters. Apparently, after the next conflagration, Beanie Babies will give the survivors in Wisconsin the most comfort.

Both Rush Limbaugh and Ann Coulter score pretty high among Wyoming residents. Those are the two celebrities googled most often in the Cowboy state. Bill O'Reilly is more popular in Montana, in case you were wondering.

Speaking of celebrities, which state residents do you suppose look up Elvis most often? Right: Tennessee. And

Tennessee men are most interested in determining whether their wives are cheating.

Alabama has it in for President Obama. Alabamans combine the name Obama most often with antichrist and impeach in their Google searches. By the way, Kentucky residents tie Alabama for anti-Obama sentiments.

When it comes to politics, District of Columbia residents seem to be multi-partisan. They search the Republican Party, the Democratic Party, Hillary Clinton, and Ronald Reagan. Can't be more even-handed than that.

Colorado residents are interested in marijuana, of course, along with the preferred food to satisfy the munchies that is a by-product of pot. In Colorado, apparently it's Rocky Mountain Oysters.

West Virginia isn't as interested in marijuana as it is in how to make moonshine.

Guess which state's residents search "How to roll a joint" and growing marijuana most often? No, not California. It's Maine.

Maryland has a thing for David Hasselhoff and for crabs, but I won't leap to the obvious conclusion.

Alaskans are curious about Sarah Palin and mail order brides, not in that order.

If you happen to be in Florida and you're online, you can easily be searching alligator wrestling and Viagra. Louisianans are also interested in wrestling alligators, but apparently don't need to research Viagra.

I would have thought that shuffleboard would be high on the list for Floridians, but it's Nebraska seniors who googles shuffleboard most often.

Residents of Illinois want to know about pizza, deep dish pizza, thin crust pizza, and burritos. You'd think marijuana was legal in that state.

Unlike Georgia, which googles butt implants, Nevada residents google breast implants. They also often need to know how to remove tattoos, so what happens in Las Vegas doesn't always stay in Las Vegas.

From the statistics involving Google searches, it can be inferred that Michigan is the capital of knock-knock jokes.

When it comes to bed bugs and handover remedies, New York is the place to google those topics.

Estately.com has provided a wonderful service to those of us who are curious about what others are curious about.

Springs

My daughter and son-in-law live in Silver Spring, Maryland. Silver Spring is a town with more than 70,000 residents, so living in that town is not unusual. What is surprising is that everyone who lives there refers to their community as "Silver Spring" and just about everyone else in the world refers to it as "Silver *Springs*."

That got me thinking. How many other towns have the singular version of the word "spring" in them?

There's a Spring City, Pennsylvania, a Spring City, Utah, and a Spring, Texas, not to be confused with Big Spring, Texas.

We also have Spring Hill, Tennessee and, yes, Spring City in the same state. Kansas also has a city called Spring Hill. Illinois has Spring Valley. And Michigan has Spring Lake.

There's a Spring City Cycling Club, but it's in Huntsville, Alabama. And speaking of cycling clubs, the Spring City Spinners Bicycle Club is located in Waukesha, Wisconsin, also home to the Spring City Trolley. There's also a Spring Green in Wisconsin.

How about the City of Spring Park, which may also be called Spring Lake Park, both in Minnesota, but clearly distinguished from Spring Lake, North Carolina. In addition to Spring Park and Spring Lake Park, Minnesota also has Cold Spring and Spring Valley, which they may have stolen from Illinois, and Spring Grove.

But none of those Spring-like cities, hills, lakes, and trolleys is likely to be mispronounced like Silver Spring,

Maryland is. Maybe that's because they have the word, "Spring" as the first part of their name.

As I was researching cities and towns with the singular "Spring" in their names, I came across dozens of towns and cities with plural "Springs." As much as I'd like to, I'm not going to bore you anymore than I already have by listing all or even some of them.

Be grateful that most of you don't live in Minnesota, where it must be perpetually difficult to deal with spring fever.

Traveling with Tchaikovsky

As I've mentioned more than once, I dislike traveling. Maybe "dislike" is too weak a word. I detest traveling, hate traveling, abhor, despise, loathe, anathematize... okay, I've gone too far, but you get my drift.

For me, the only thing worse than traveling is traveling by air. The experience is dreadful, from beginning to end, from the TSA folks who insist that I remove my jacket, my shoes, my keys, my wallet, and the facial tissues in my pockets before boarding the plane, to the seats into which only an anorexic six-year-old can squeeze, to the overhead storage that is one eighth of an inch too small for my carry-on bag, to the flight attendant who demands my attention so I can refresh myself with the intricacies of operating my seatbelt, to the kid in the row behind me whose feet play an unending tarantella on my seatback while her baby brother shrieks his lungs out the entire trip, to the ride itself, complete with unpredictable, precipitous drops in altitude, each of which, in my mind, portends the beginning of a death spiral, to the exploded remnants of my recently-purchased matching luggage that appear, if at all, on the baggage carousel.

And don't get me started on the cuisine. As Woody Allen once said, the food is terrible and the portions are too small.

You can imagine my skepticism, then, a short time ago when I boarded a Delta Airlines flight to a much colder and less hospitable place than south Florida, and was presented with earbuds or in-ear headphones while we taxied to a runway. For starters, earbuds are meant to be inserted *into* one's ears. This is in sharp contrast to the headphones I notice first class travelers get for only three times the cost of my seat in steerage. First class headphones, you see, come with foam cushioning so that they can be gently positioned against the outside of one's ears, not in them.

But I shouldn't quibble. The earbuds were provided without charge and I never refuse anything free, except at *Fiery José's*, my neighborhood Mexican restaurant whose fork tines, over the years, have all melted from the heat of the enchiladas. Although the extra hot sauce is free, I've learned discretion is much better than ingesting it.

Now back to my flight. After placing the earbuds in my ears, I reached down to the front of my arm rest to rotate the channel selector to classical music. By that time, our plane's engines were revving up.

And then the magic happened. Just as the pilot released the brakes and the plane began to progress down the runway, I heard the first notes of Tchaikovsky's *Piano Concerto No. 1*. You know, the one that begins with the French horns announcing the piece like an orchestra version of the first call bugle at a race track.

I wouldn't blame you if you don't believe this next part, because I hardly do myself, and I was there. With uncanny timing, the pianist started his chords and then the whole orchestra came in with the first theme just as the plane's tires left the pavement and we lifted off.

The music crescendoed and the relentless chords acted like prodigious impulses, I felt, thrusting the plane ever upward into the sky. The continuous building of musical tension matched the roaring, powerful jet engines propelling us heavenward.

I've never come that close to having an orgasm to a piece of music, and yes, that includes Ravel's *Bolero*. Now don't tell me you haven't all tried that.

As the plane began to bank, I turned in my seat to see if people behind me were listening to the same piece of music. I would know by their euphoric expressions.

But no, I was apparently the only passenger on the plane who witnessed this incredible juxtaposition of heavenly music and soaring power. You couldn't time the music to the flight better in a hundred years.

I tell you, if I could be assured of this happy coincidence every time, it could make a traveler out of me.

Your Right to Reverse

Cars today are marvels of technology. Some have a mind of their own. The latest models have sensors to detect obstacles and people as you back up. The car applies your brakes automatically before you collide with any person or thing you may not be able to see in your rearview mirror.

It's an interesting concept that can be really valuable and I'm sure a lot of highly-paid engineers spent many sleepless nights working out the complicated details.

There's only one major problem as far as I can see. It's not a mechanical problem, not an electrical problem nor an optical problem; it's a legal problem: those back-up sensors connected to the brakes are unconstitutional.

Oh sure, you don't want to hit a fire hydrant or another car in a parking lot — especially if it's a low-slung, shiny, new Lamborghini. Those babies sell for a minimum of between a third and a half million dollars and I shudder to think how much their front bumper or a headlight costs to replace.

On the other hand, certain obstacles deserve to be run over, like the tricycle that belongs to that incredibly hyperactive, noisy kid with terminal attention deficit disorder who lives next door. How else can you get even with him for waking you up at 6:00 a.m. every morning for the last week?

How can you get even with the annoying team of garbage men — oops, sanitation engineers — who take delight in abruptly cracking the silence of the neighborhood with their cacophonous symphony of garbage cans and lids thrown against their trucks and then unceremoniously tossed from what sounds like a great height onto the sidewalk at 8:22 every Saturday morning? How can you get even? Well, you can lie in wait in your car in the driveway at 8:20 hoping to back up into one of them and maybe break his lid-tossing arm.

How about this? What if you happen to be Bond — James Bond — and a sadistic, vicious, murderous spy from the other side is creeping up behind your Aston Martin DB5? You'll miss a great opportunity to take care of the scoundrel because your car insists on slamming on the brakes just when the movie music swells to a climax and you goose the gas pedal.

"But Mark," I can hear you protest, "I'm not James Bond and nefarious spies never sneak up on me from the rear or from the front, either."

Okay, you want to be more realistic? It doesn't have to be an innocent tricycle or your ex-wife's lawyer or an inconsiderate garbage man or a homicidal maniac you may wish to dispatch.

Maybe it's your mother-in-law.

Do you want some automobile manufacturer depriving you of a once-in-a-lifetime chance to accidentally rid the world of a person so evil she has made your life a living hell for the past 12 years by calling daily and visiting when you least expect it or want it, and inciting your children to ask for games and toys way beyond your means or — worse yet — actually buying drum sets for those same irresponsible kids?

I didn't think so.

In fact, I think there's something in the Constitution that prohibits car makers from abridging your right to take matters into your own hands when you feel like it. I'll have to look it up, but I believe it's part of the Second Amendment.

In any event, my word of caution is: before you purchase a new car with a back-up sensor and automatic braking, be sure it comes with a shutoff switch, even if it costs a few bucks more.

IV

YOU CALL THIS WORK?

Autodidacts

Autodidacts, as all of us with college educations know, are people who have been partially or wholly self-taught. You may have heard of some of them.

For example, among writers, Jorge Luis Borges was an autodidact.

Hermann Hesse won the Nobel Prize for literature, and so did Jose Saramago, who had to abandon college because he ran out of money. So did Rabindranath Tagore, the Bengali fellow who was the first non-European to win the Nobel Prize. So did Ernest Hemingway, who was primarily self-educated after high school, reading for hours at a time in bed. He might have used bigger words if he had attended college, but who am I to criticize?

Harlan Ellison attended Ohio State University for 18 months before being expelled for hitting a professor who criticized his writing. For the following 40 years he sent the professor a copy of every work he published. Ahh, revenge is sweet, ain't it, Harlan?

H.P. Lovecraft was a self-taught writer who attended school only in brief stints, since his health problems hounded him his whole life.

Maxim Gorky, Sir Terry Pratchett, and Herman Melville didn't bother to stay in school either, once they learned how to type.

George Bernard Shaw left formal education, comparing schools to prison. Those are the harshest words I've ever heard from a vegetarian pacifist.

Louis L'Amour left his home at the age of 15 to expand his horizons. He worked many jobs while educating himself.

Ray Bradbury did not attend college, saying, "libraries raised me. I don't believe in colleges and universities." But ironically, they sure believe in him. Bradbury's stories and novels are required reading in many schools.

L. Ron Hubbard started out as a science fiction writer and then founded the Church of Scientology. Maybe you don't need formal education if God has your ear.

Great writers aren't the only ones who succeeded without a sheepskin. A number of actors, musicians, and other artist are in that untutored boat.

Claudio Arrau was highly regarded as an intellectual despite his lack of formal education outside his musical training. Arrau spoke five languages that he learned on his own.

Frank Zappa said, "Drop out of school before your mind rots from exposure to our mediocre educational system." But I liked him anyway.

Some filmmakers dropped out of college or film school, including Orson Welles, Stanley Kubrick, John Huston, Woody Allen, Roman Polanski, Quentin Tarantino, James Cameron, and — wait for it — even Steven Spielberg.

Craig Ferguson quit high school in his native Scotland at the minimum legal age: 16.

The magic team of Penn & Teller are both autodidacts who may have taught each other to say, "abracadabra."

Keith Moon, the drummer for the rock band *The Who*, is one of the greatest drummers of all time, but had only three or four drum lessons with Carlo Little, an early member of the *Rolling Stones*, who was also a self-taught drummer.

David Bowie had a few singing lessons, but basically taught himself to play the saxophone, the piano, the harmonica, the bass, percussion, the electric and acoustic guitar, and the synthesizer. He also taught himself painting, sculpture, dance, and mime. No wonder he had no time for school.

Both Jimi Hendrix and Kurt Cobain taught themselves how to play guitar.

Eminem dropped out of high school at age 17 and had to repeat ninth grade a few times. He said his ability to rhyme came from reading the dictionary front to back multiple times to expand his vocabulary. Yes, that would do it.

Malcolm X copied a dictionary word-for-word while in prison for seven years.

Errol Flynn and Noël Coward didn't get beyond high school. Beat that, Dick Cavett.

Frank Lloyd Wright, who thought a lot of himself, apparently didn't think too much of formal education. But along with womanizing, he taught himself architecture.

Career Advice

When I was barely a teenager, as clueless about my future as most teenagers whose parents are not physicians, I took some career aptitude tests. I had always done well on academic aptitude tests that featured math problems. Notice, I said "well," not phenomenally well.

But even at the tender age of 13, I realized that the number of professions for which solving elementary math problems was required couldn't be very large. I mean, I had never heard of one, except for my seventh grade math teacher, and he had weird taste in neckties — weird even by math nerd standards.

Anyway, there came that point in my life when I realized I had to get serious about my future. It was stressful not knowing the direction I should be going. Not so stressful that it was affecting my appetite, of course, I wasn't obsessed, but I was stressed enough to think about my situation every week or two. My ever-helpful parents arranged for me to take a couple of hours of aptitude tests.

Here's the strange thing: when my test results were analyzed, the counselor recommended that I consider a career in ... fashion design. Fashion design! I — who couldn't tell the difference between culottes and mu mus and couldn't care less — I become a fashion designer?

It wasn't until years later that I realized the counselor was somehow motivated to direct students to attend a particular fashion school, regardless of their lack of aptitude or interest.

That experience was not entirely a waste of time, although I thought so for the last 50 years. The fact is, though, I scored highest n the subject called academic research aptitude. That's not the same as scientific research, by the way.

In any case, I had no interest in becoming a librarian, so I filed that factoid away until recently, when I had an epiphany of sorts. It turns out I *am* good at academic research — research on the Internet. I look up information eight or ten times a day.

It seems like every other minute I'm confirming how words are spelled or I'm locating appropriate synonyms.

For these *Weekend Radio* essays, I have researched not-so-famous national days, like National Talk like a Pirate Day, and the number of people in America named Roy Rogers, and people and things whose acronym is R.C., and which famous people were born on my birthday. I've discovered that lobsters are related to cockroaches and that Marilyn Monroe's last, incomplete movie also featured Dean Martin.

I use the search engine, Google, and the Internet tells me that word, spelled correctly — g-o-o-g-o-l — was made popular by Edward Kasner, who used it in his book, *MATHEMATICS AND THE IMAGINATION*, published in 1940.

It means one followed by 100 zeroes, which is actually called ten duo-tri-gintillion, if you care.

Anyway, thanks to the Google Internet search engine, I can retrieve pretty much anything I want to know by typing in two or three words. My talent — and I have to refer to talent with a lower case "t" — comes in useful for those trivial purposes I mentioned as well as for searching patented inventions on the Patent and Trademark Office database.

Of course, the Internet database didn't exist when I was informed that I had academic research aptitude.

So even though I don't get to solve simple math problems for a living, at least I was spared from a life of fashion design.

Dying to Work

Most of the time, I feel sorry for past and present presidents of the United States, even the ones I didn't vote for. They have a difficult job, and it shows. After four or eight years, they visibly age. There are more wrinkles, stress, and gray hair in photographs of them before and after their terms of office. One expert said that while they're in office, presidents tend to age twice as fast as non-presidents. I guess that's good news and bad news, if you want to be president.

Being president means there's about a 10% chance that you will be killed before your term is up. During the history of the United States, eight presidents have died in office. Of those eight, four were assassinated and four died from natural causes. More about dying at work in a minute.

William Harrison, our ninth U.S. president, holds the record for shortest term served, holding the office of presidency for 31 days before dying of pneumonia, which he contracted at his chilly inauguration. He gave the longest inauguration speech in history. Someone should have suggested he wear a hat, overcoat, and gloves that wet, freezing January day in Washington, but I'm guessing most of the audience had nodded off.

Zachary Taylor died from acute gastroenteritis. He was the first president to be elected with no prior office. The first, but not the last, as we now know.

Warren G. Harding suffered a heart attack and died at the age of 57. He is consistently ranked the worst president, but at least he made the record books for something. There's no such thing as bad publicity, as they say.

Franklin D. Roosevelt married Eleanor, who didn't have to change her name, because she was a niece of President Theodore Roosevelt. So she was his fifth cousin, once removed. I mention that because it's the sort of useless trivia you've come to expect from my ramblings. Anyway, FDR collapsed and died as a result of a cerebral hemorrhage at the beginning of his fourth term as president.

I recently looked up how long presidents live after they retire and found some surprising statistics. Six presidents lived into their nineties: John Adams, Herbert Hoover, Ronald Reagan, Gerald Ford, George H.W. Bush, and Jimmy Carter. That's about 13%. To put that in perspective, nowadays, if you were born after the year 2010, you have a 20% chance of living to at least 90, but of course you don't have a 20% chance of becoming president.

Five presidents lived into their eighties. That's a pretty good percentage of octogenarians and nonagenarians out of 45 presidents. In fact, the average lifespan for the first eight presidents was 79.8 years in an era when the average man died before 40.

Excluding assassinations, only two presidents didn't make it to the age of 60. James Polk wanted to be president for just one term and he succeeded. During his short presidency, the U.S. acquired California, Oregon, and, via the Mexican American war, eventually acquired the great state of Texas. He increased U.S. real estate by about a third. Not a bad record for the person known as the "least known consequential president." He died of cholera at the age of 53, three months after leaving office, having had the shortest retirement of any U.S. president.

Chester Arthur was 57 when he died. He, along with James Polk, decided one term – actually only 3 1/2 years, since he took over from assassinated President James Garfield – was enough. Shortly after becoming president, Arthur was diagnosed with Bright's disease, a kidney ailment now referred to as nephritis. But that didn't kill him. He died from a cerebral hemorrhage a year after he left office.

The moral of the story is, if you'd like to have a good chance of living a long life, just become president of the United States.

On the other hand – and there's always another hand, isn't there? – an orchestra conductor may not be your best choice for living a long life. Sure, Pablo Casals, Nadia Boulanger, Stokowski, and Toscanini all lived into their nineties. Conductor Blanche Honnegger Moyse even lived to the whopping age of 102. Wikipedia has a nice list of musical centenarians. And sure, the list of octogenarians includes Sir Thomas Beecham, Eugene Ormandy, Bruno Walter, Ernest Ansermet, Walter Damrosch, Arthur Fiedler, and Pierre Monteux.

But how about all those conductors who died early and, in fact, died at work in an orchestra pit or on a podium? At least 14 of them died like that. I won't bore you with the details of all of their demises, since you can find them on the Internet. But here are a few to warn you of what orchestral pieces to stay away from when you become the conductor of a major orchestra.

Giuseppe Sinopoli, head of Dresden's Staatskapelle and former head of the Philharmonia Orchestra in London, died at the age of only 54. Another Giuseppe who was slated to head the Rome Opera. His name was Giuseppe Patane and he died at the age of 57 while conducting The Barber of Seville in Munich.

Felix Mottl was 56 when he collapsed and died while conducting Tristan und Isolde.

Eduard van Beinum was 58 when he died during a rehearsal of Brahms's First Symphony.

Franz Konwitshny was 60 and former head of the Dresden Opera. He died while rehearsing Beethoven's Missa Solemnis. True, he was a heavy drinker and some people even called him Kon-whisky, so Beethoven wasn't his only vice.

Dimitri Mitropoulos, conductor of the New York Philharmonic, collapsed and died at the age of 64 while rehearsing Mahler's Third Symphony.

So you see, being a musical conductor doesn't guarantee a long life. You're better off being president. I know that's where I'm heading.

First Day on the Job

If you're lucky enough to be hired, especially if it's your first job or your first new job in a while, I have a few words of advice: don't show up for work. At least not on a Monday. Ironically, that's the most popular day of the week to start a new job, but it's the absolute worst option.

Here's why.

When you start a new job, you are expected to learn trivial as well as important new tasks. Depending on how complicated the job, getting up to speed might take a huge amount of concentration and significant time, neither of which you will want to expend on the first day following your last weekend of freedom. I, myself, have never applied for a position that requires huge concentration, so I can't really speak from experience. But I can imagine what a headache that must be.

Also, you will have to remember all the people you meet, four of whom inevitably will have such similar names as Laurie, Lora, Lauren, and Linda. And yes, they're all the same height, the same age, and all wear glasses.

Keeping all those people straight in your mind can be a full time job in itself. Even though I haven't met them, I'm so ready for a vacation, just thinking about all those human alliterations or, for you etymologists, all those lambdacisms.

You will also have to keep track of important places around your new cubicle, including but not limited to the location your boss's cubicle, the coffee break room, the supply closet, the mailroom, the smoking area, the receiving department, and — last but not least important — the location of the restroom. You'll have to learn where overnight packages are delivered and, believe me — here I *am* speaking from experience — overnight packages are never delivered to the mailroom or even close to it.

You will have to go to Human Resources to show your driver's license and social security card, sign a dozen papers and attend a briefing, then to Security for a badge and a parking space and another briefing, and then to Compensation to sign even more papers and, of course, yet another briefing. You'll have to tell people how many dependents you have, how much of your pay you'd like to put into the stock plan, how much you'd like to donate to a local community fund, whether you want to be paid weekly, bi-weekly, or semi-monthly.

Since cash payments are pretty much frowned on nowadays, to say nothing of getting paid in gold bullion or Spanish doubloons, you will have to decide whether your pay should be deposited automatically in your bank account or whether you'd prefer receiving a check, except, of course, on the third Thursday of every fourth month when Doris from Payroll visits her mother in a convalescent home outside of Santa Fe ever since she (the mother, not Doris) had that stroke that debilitated her six years ago when her house burned under what police called suspicious circumstances.

You'll also have to declare which insurance plan your spouse has, which company plan you wish to participate in, and, of course, your non-spouse next of kin along with his or her social security number, addresses and phone numbers, both home and work.

So you see, you'll have to answer a host of questions that first day. As the day grinds on like an unending Wagnerian opera, a ton of questions will also probably form in your mind. But here's another hint: try not to ask too many questions in the beginning because you'll be expected to remember the answers and — let's face it — most of the answers don't matter, anyway.

When you get home, you'll be so exhausted, you'll feel like skipping dinner and going directly to bed way before the sun sets.

The next day at work will be better, but still challenging. You should have time for a few dry or wet runs to the restroom, you'll be meeting yet more people whose names start with "L," and you'll be learning ever more complicated tasks. By the end of the second day, you'll be beyond fatigued; you'll be nearly comatose.

That's why I suggest you don't start to work on a Monday with five long, terror-filled days ahead of you. You can give your new boss a believable excuse like you're superstitious when Jupiter is in Aquarius. Or your cat, Murray, has a standing appointment with his veterinarian psychologist. Or you belong to an obscure religious sect that happens to celebrate a holiday that Monday with non-fat cottage cheese. Or that Monday is the funeral for your pet turtle, Timmy, who perished in a suspicious fire outside of Santa Fe. You get the idea.

Do whatever you have to in order to start work on a Thursday, if possible, or a Wednesday at the earliest. That way you can have the weekend to recuperate.

You can try to remember some of the ten thousand new things you've been forced to learn. And you can contemplate what the heck you've gotten yourself into.

Here's Some Advice: Take My Advice!

As I started to think about the most important advice I ever received, I realized that I had a lot to choose from. I've received advice in at least six languages, including English. *Carpe diem* (Latin), seize the day; *répondez s'il vous plaît* (French), please respond; ¡*vamanos!* (Spanish), let's go; *mach schnell* (German), shake a leg; and *sheket be'vakasha* (Hebrew), please shut up.

My mother taught me to put my napkin on my lap, not to chew with my mouth open, not to speak with my mouth full, not to place my elbows on the table, and not to use the big fork for salad. All that advice was just for breakfast.

Speaking of food, the late L. Rust Hills in *How to do Things Right* advised parents never to allow their children to enter the family car with an ice cream cone. Not only will the interior of your car become permanently sticky, but with what seems like a violation of the laws of nature, so will every other car you buy.

Mel Brooks, playing the 2,000 year old man, attributed the secret to his longevity to never, ever running for a bus.

It's been a while since I saw *Fatal Attraction*, the movie in which Glen Close played an obsessed woman who had a sexual affair with Michael Douglas' character. But I overheard two little old ladies in front of me as I walked out of the movie theater.

"Hope you learned a lesson, boys," said one of them to a couple of teenagers ahead of them.

"Yeah," replied one of the boys. "Never use your right name."

At my wedding, my father told me, "it's easy to criticize." To this day, I don't know if that was a warning or merely an observation.

When I started working in upstate New York in 1983, I was lucky enough to overlap my predecessor, Gerry, for a week. Gerry had been with the company for 40 years. I knew I could gain a great deal of knowledge about the job and the company from him. So when I asked him for advice, I was happy that he was willing to comply. He held up his hand with three fingers extended.

"Three?" I said, expecting a short game of Charades. I leaned forward in anticipation of his words of wisdom.

Gerry nodded. Here was his advice: "It's very rainy here, so you'll need three umbrellas: one at your home, one at the office, and one in your car."

Sometimes, the advice is flat wrong.

For example, a camp counselor explained the facts of life to my 10-year-old bunkmates and me one summer. He advised us not to have sexual relations with a woman when she was in the fertile portion of her menstrual cycle. I learned, some years later, that he was confused. The days he identified as the infertile portion of the cycle were, in fact, the fertile days. Oops.

And speaking of dangerous blunders in the advice department, a newspaper in the Pacific Northwest once thought it prudent to inform its readers that the caption below respective mushroom photographs the week before were inadvertently switched. The poisonous mushroom, it turned out, should have been identified as the photo on the left page.

James Bond advised that martinis should be shaken, but I have since learned that a martini is actually colder if it is stirred in ice, preferably at least 50 times.

So here's my advice: don't believe everything you read or hear; sometimes advice can be wrong, even when it comes from an otherwise reputable source. And who would be more reputable than old double oh seven?

As Oscar Wilde might have said, "don't believe every bit of advice anyone gives you. That includes mine, especially."

I Work Too Hard

I don't know about you, but I think I work too hard. On average, I go to my office eight hours a day, five days a week, if you can believe that. Man, that's 40 hours per week, minus some time for lunch, of course, and coffee breaks, birthday celebrations, anniversaries, and Monday morning quarter-backing.

Now that I think of it, the expression I used, "work too hard," may not be entirely accurate. After all, pushing pencils and pounding keyboards doesn't qualify as hard manual labor. It's not as if we white collar workers actually sweat, unless we're being interviewed by an IRS agent.

But still, doing anything for 40 hours per week seems too long — really excessive. So it's not that my work is too hard, exactly, as much as too long. If I put my mind to it and I weren't working, in a 40 hour week I could watch about 24 feature length movies, or I could prepare 600 peanut butter and jelly sandwiches, or I could brush my teeth 800 times. Gives me a different perspective on what 40 hours really means.

I know some people would love to work *only* 40 hours per week — people with second jobs, for instance. I've even heard of some folks who work up to 100 hours every week, which doesn't leave much time for playing golf, preparing chocolate soufflés or doing inconsequential things, like sleeping.

The 40 hour work week has been our standard for 70 years, since 1938, when Congress, during Franklin Roosevelt's administration, passed the Fair Labor Standards Act as part of the New Deal to help eliminate sweatshops. By the way, 1938 was also the year that oil was discovered in Saudi Arabia, but I guess that's an essay for another time.

Under the Fair Labor Standards Act, time working beyond 40 hours was to be compensated at at least one and a half times the regular rate of pay, so employers would be dissuaded from forcing their employees to work too long. Ironically, nowadays many of us look forward to working overtime to make ends meet. In fact, over three fifths of us in America work more than 40 hours a week, and 40% of us work more than 50 hours a week. Let's face it, the cost of ingredients for chocolate soufflés is increasing all the time, to say nothing about the cost of Saudi oil.

About 50 years ago, in 1961, a published prediction[*], presumably by a reputable source, said that by now the standard work week would be only 29 hours long. That prediction also included the belief that 5% of the world's population would be living in space, that common colds and cancer would be eliminated, and that, by now, cars would float on air, being powered by engines the size of a typewriter. Predictions don't always come true, I guess, so I'm not banking on a four-hour work week, as recently predicted for Generation Y people by a woman named Penelope Trunk.[**]

There was a concern a few years back that we workers wouldn't know what to do with all of our free time. Of course, that was before the invention of reality T.V. shows.

The point is, we've had the 40 hour week standard for the better part of a century now. Isn't it time that Congress adjusted it downwardly to — oh, I don't know — maybe to the number of hours Congress itself works on those rare occasions when it's in session?

------

[*]   www.pixelmatic.com.au/2000/
[**] http://blog.penelopetrunk.com/2007/12/12/ the-end-of-work-as-we-know-it/

Let's Dance

At the last wedding I attended, I was strongly encouraged to join a number of revelers on the dance floor. Having never taken a dance lesson from a professional instructor, I've always been self-conscious about moving about and awkwardly gesticulating in public to the beat of a band.

But I've learned from watching others on the dance floor. I can gyrate my upper body, bounce my head, and flail my arms with the best of them, but I've also learned the most important part: to keep my feet planted as the song progresses. I've found that moving my upper body and my lower body simultaneously is very strenuous. At the conclusion of the exercise, I desire nothing so much as a nap, which turns out to be problematical due to the clangorous noises the band is inflicting on us undeserving guests. Not that I haven't tried to nap as the festivities drone on, but I'm also afraid I'll sleep through dessert, the high point of most celebrations.

I did notice last month no one else was doing much better than I was on the dance floor. The men, especially, appeared to be as clueless as I was.

Look how far we've come from, say, the 19th century, when everyone knew how to waltz, if not minuet. In movies depicting that period you just don't see dancers wandering around like you do today with their arms in the air and a vacant expression on their faces.

Dances in the old, old days seemed to have a purpose and a structure. In fact, even as recently as the 1950s, Fred Astaire and Gene Kelly appeared in movies with graceful, decisive moves. They were in absolute control. No stepping on their partners' toes or taking off in the wrong direction or panting for breath. Viewers probably thought the Astaires and Kellys would last forever, but the dance scene changes from generation to generation and Fred and Gene are now relegated to old movies.

At the turn of the last century, the Tango made its way up from Argentina, followed by the Merengue, the Samba, the Mambo, the Rumba, and the Cha Cha. And of course in the 1920s, the Charleston was the cat's meow.

In the '40s, '50s, and '60s, we had many names for dances. Sometimes the name was the most creative part of the dance. We all remember the Twist, the Loco-Motion, the Lindy, the Jitterbug, and the Mashed Potato. Some of us tried to Frug, to Swim, to Limbo, and to Pony. Before that, every self-respecting wedding band had to include a Bunny Hop and a Hokey Pokey along with a Polka or Hora, depending on the wedding couple's ethnic persuasion.

The disco movement arrived in the 1970s with dances like the Bump, the Hustle, and the YMCA.

The Chicken Dance made its appearance in the '80s in America, usually performed by the bride's cute-as-a-button uncle. It was originally called the Duck Dance when Werner Thomas composed it on his accordion in the 1950s in Switzerland and encouraged dancers to flap their wings and shake their tail feathers.

The song, *Walk Like an Egyptian* came out about the same time and, to me, seemed a lot more sophisticated in comparison.

The Macarena in the early '90s was recorded by a one-hit wonder, Los Del Rio, and was released as a Rumba. The nice thing about the Macarena was a dancer like me could check out what the person next to him was doing and sort of keep up.

More recently the Gangnam Style dance was popular for what seemed like a decade, but was actually less than a year.

Gangnam Style is a louder, more violent version of the Pony. It became the first YouTube video to reach one billion views within a few months after being introduced in July, 2012.

Twerking seemed the thing to do after Miley Cyrus performed at the *Video Music Awards* in March, 2013. I haven't seen any amateurs do this dance yet, but then again I'm never invited to the types of parties that feature that dance. If I tried to twerk now, I'd end up in the Emergency Room. Anyway, it's not the sort of dance movement grandparents approve of.

I never learned how to Crocodile Rock or Watusi, either. Those and almost 100 other fad dances appeared on the rock and roll scene in the '60s. They included Achy Breaky Heart, the Creep, the Fly, and Peanut Butter Jelly Time. Those were the heydays of dances of the month and I miss them, although I don't think my knees do.

I haven't even mentioned ballroom dances and line dances, as you may have noticed.

But for now it's off to another wedding and I'm planning to cut a rug, whatever that means.

Not-So-Starving Artists

You've heard the expression, "starving artist." It refers to a person who performs or paints or composes or writes poetry, mostly, and if he earns money at all, he barely pays his bills. He may not be starving, but he certainly isn't getting fat ordering garlic mashed potatoes with his surf and turf at *Morton's Steakhouse*.

An example of a starving artist is Vincent Van Gogh, the great Dutch artist who shot himself to death at the age of 38 and who, in his lifetime, had sold only one or maybe two of his 2,000 paintings, which included 860 oil paintings. In a three-year period alone, he knocked out 37 self-portraits. Some of his paintings have sold recently for $100 million apiece, give or take. Ah, if he had only doubled his life span. Timing, as we say in the art biz, is everything.

Another starving artist was Wolfgang Amadeus Mozart, the prolific composer who created 600 musical works. He also died at a premature age, but not before he composed music that has since been incorporated in some 200 movies. In addition to *Elvira Madigan,* movies that feature his music include but are not limited to *Amadeus, American Gigolo, Anne Frank, The Associate, Babette's Feast, Barry Lyndon, Batman, A Beautiful Mind, The Big Lebowski, The Bonfire of the Vanities, Bridget Jones's Diary,* and *Ace Ventura: Pet Detective.* And those are just the movies with titles beginning with the letters, A and B. Wolfgang died at the ripe age of 35 and in debt, and was buried in a common grave.

It's more than a little depressing to dwell on talented artists who were not recognized for their contributions during their lifetimes. I'd rather focus on the exceptions to the starving artist rule.

Take Gioachino Rossini, for example. He was known as the Italian Mozart, but a lot more successful during his life. In addition to the *Lone Ranger Overture* that he composed for Clayton Moore and Jay Silverheels, he wrote about 40 operas, and retired at only 38. In his retirement, he established his reputation as an amateur chef and a corpulent gourmand. At his death in 1878, his estate was valued at well over a million dollars, which is hi ho and away impressive now, to say nothing of 136 years ago. Gioachino was anything but a starving artist.

Pablo Picasso is another artist who made it big during his lifetime. Picasso constructed a Gothic home and three large villas on the French Riviera. He was commissioned to make a maquette for a public sculpture to be built in Chicago, known as the 50-foot-high *Chicago Picasso*. For that sculpture, one of the most recognizable landmarks in downtown Chicago, Picasso declined his $100,000 fee, but donated it to the people of the city. The number of his works has been estimated at 50,000, comprising almost 2,000 paintings and thousands of prints, tapestries, and rugs. He also has the distinction of having more of his paintings stolen than any other artist. Towards the end of his life, as a world-famous artist, his local wine merchant and local bakery refused to cash Picasso's checks, since his autograph was worth more than the face value of the checks. His estate was estimated to be a quarter of a billion dollars and you have to wonder how much of that was due to bottles of wine he didn't pay for.

Salvador Dali was reputed to be worth $10 million before he died, part of which sum came from over 100,000 canvases he signed in blank so others could pass off their paintings as authentic Dalis once he passed on and only the persistence of memory remained of Salvador.

Andy Warhol left 4,000 paintings and 66,000 photographs. His estate was valued at $220 million, which works out to about 172 million Campbell cans of tomato soup.

Ernest Hemingway had accumulated over a million dollars' worth of stocks that made up his estate, believing, apparently, it's better to have than to have not.

Michael Jackson's estate was worth only $7 million when he passed away, according to his executors, but the IRS still charged the estate $700 million in back taxes. Luckily, Michael Jackson earned over $1 billion the year after he died. So now his heirs can tell the IRS to beat it.

Elvis Presley's home is visited by more people than any other private home in America, except the White House. Elvis earned $100 million during his life, but had only a measly $5 million in his bank when he died, which still could have bought a lot of blue suede shoes.

There's great consolation thinking that these essays, like Van Gogh's, may be worth more after I'm dead. Under the circumstances, though, that ain't saying much.

Successful Writers' Secrets

This year's *Best American Mystery Stories* anthology just arrived in the mail. In addition to the 20 best stories themselves, this issue of *Best American Mystery Stories* includes short biographical notes about the authors. I decided to read the bios first, since my attention span is even shorter than a short story. My hope was that I could find something most published mystery writers have in common. This would give me a clue as to what makes a writer successful. Needless to say, I had an ulterior motive for learning and applying that secret.

Sure enough, the answer leapt out at me like a bloody dagger at a crime scene. A number of authors stated they are married and have a son or daughter. The writers who didn't mention the number of children they had might have had more or less than one kid apiece. Whatever the case, they decided not to mention that fact in their bio. Of the writers who mentioned having a family, only the ones with a single child declared themselves.

The authors had different socioeconomic backgrounds and came from different locations in the U.S. and Canada. They were ethnically diverse and represented both genders. In fact, except for writing the best stories of the year, they seemed to have nothing in common, but for the fact that some of them are the parent of an only child. I decided to investigate other writers to see how prolific they were, progeny-wise.

While Googling the topic, I discovered that Lauren Sandler, who wrote a book about children without siblings titled, ONE AND ONLY, had also already written an essay for *The Atlantic* magazine, observing that many women writers, like

Susan Sontag, Joan Didion, and Mary McCarthy, have only one child. There you have it. Ms. Sandler preempted me. And here I thought *I* was the first to discover the secret of literary success.

What a surprising but simple characteristic successful writers have in common. The key to being a proficient writer is not necessarily one's formal education, or books one reads on the writing craft, or where or when one writes every day, or how quickly one writes, or whether one prepares an outline prior to writing, or what one drinks and how much.

Success is based not only on an extraordinary ability to create a plot, or develop characters, or produce conflict, or rewrite a piece over and over and over, as I used to suspect, but merely on parenting one and only one child.

Lauren Sandler seems to think it may be that fewer children provide less of a distraction for their writer parent. Or maybe the money a person saves by raising only one child — as opposed to a bunch of them — can be used to hire a babysitter.

Of course not every famous writer followed this practice. Norman Mailer and his nine children come to mind. Now Mailer had six wives, but that still averages 1.5 children per wife. You know what they say: It's the exception that proves the rule.

Interestingly, some very good writers were only children themselves. I'm thinking of E.M. Forster, Ezra Pound, Hans Christian Anderson, John Updike, Lillian Hellman, and Jean-Paul Sartre. I'm not sure what that shows, except Google is really an excellent vehicle for discovering trivia, useful or otherwise.

This brings me to my struggle to become a famous novelist whose books are made into blockbuster Hollywood movies before they're even published. My major mistake was having too many children. I have two daughters when I should have had one.

I should have evaluated whether a fulfilling life with two or more beautiful, loving, talented, accomplished daughters outweighs a career, say, as a potential Nobel Prize-winning author. That's like saying would I rather have a cut body with an incredible six pack or be President of the United States; or would I rather have a full head of hair or be the first astronaut on Mars? It's one of my many regrets, as you can imagine, that I can't have great abs and luxurious hair and be the first President to visit Mars.

Now I can't guarantee that my life would have been different if I had limited my number of children, but at least I can fantasize where I'd be if I had only one beautiful, loving, talented, accomplished daughter instead of a backup for her.

Ah well, unless I want to jeopardize my chances for visiting Mars, it's probably too late to do anything about that now.

Why I Won't Retire

I come from a long line of ancestors who died with their boots on, and I can see why. The prospect of retirement — swaying listlessly on a rocker in a near-comatose state in front of a television set for 16 hours every day — gives me the willies.

With the way modern medicine is treating and curing people with every known disease, including old age, there's no telling how long our current generation will live. Sure, I can retire any day now, but how can I be sure I won't live another thousand years? And what then? How many times will I be required to watch reruns of *One Day at a Time*?

A lot of my friends in their 60s and even 50s are retiring now. In preparation for the big day, they obsess over only two things: moving somewhere and traveling.

Just about everyone who plans on retiring, plans on retiring somewhere else. They're looking forward to leaving the home they've lived in for years or even decades, the home in which their children grew up, the home that has a healthy crab apple tree on the front lawn where they planted a scrawny sapling only 36 years earlier. They're planning on saying good-bye to loads of friends and neighbors, to the mailman and to that guy behind the seafood counter who they can finally trust when he talks about the freshness of the cod or the salmon.

Now some of my friends have thought this out and are moving to warmer, quieter communities. Most of them are downsizing, moving to gated developments with one- or two-bedroom apartments, not so much for physical security as to discourage overly-long visits from their children and grandchildren, God bless them.

That all makes sense. But what about those who are moving just because they're supposed to move? Some of them are so desperate, they're moving to places that are clearly less appealing than the place they're moving from. The urge to change residences, like lemmings' urge to plunge off a cliff to the sea, seems to be the only explanation for why older people would move from anywhere to, say, Cleveland.

I'm thinking that there's only one solution to the problem of forced relocation: don't retire in the first place!

Now, once the recent retirees land at their new retirement location, the place at which — let's face it — they eventually expect to die, they usually plan to escape, at least for days at a time. Yes folks, the very next step after moving to Arizona, Florida or southern California, is to take a trip. Oh, the joys of traveling as an octogenarian. It's exhausting just thinking about it.

I'm so looking forward to taking long naps when I reach that golden time close to the terminal age of Sir Winston Churchill, Bob Hope, and oh, I don't know... Mic Jagger.

When I'm 92, no one will fault me for taking a siesta in the middle of the afternoon. After all, I worked hard up to then and I deserve a little shut-eye. No, retirement is not for me. I'm planning to get some well-deserved rest and the only way to do that is not to retire.

Acknowledgements

I owe a great debt to my Wilkes University creative writing cohort and to all the friends, teachers, writers, and editors who guided and encouraged me along the way. Or at least didn't discourage me.

My mother taught me to use keyboards — piano and typewriter. My father taught me many lessons in life, including how to use a slide rule. Now that I think of it, slide rules and typewriters are obsolete artifacts of a generation or more ago. Nevertheless I still love my parents and appreciate their wisdom more every day. And when slide rules come back into fashion, I'll appreciate them even more.

Jan Quackenbush, the leader of my first creative writing group, suggested I attend graduate school even at my advanced age. Prudy Taylor Board, the leader of my Florida writing group, is never at a loss for constructive comments and, in fact, is the principal reason these essays are seeing print. Of course, all the members of both writing group help sharpen my focus, too. And "Sagebrush Bob" Conrad, an inspiration to so many in the broadcasting field, gave me a chance to voice my observations over the airwaves.

My incredibly patient friends, Matthew Nadelson, Jules Celestin, and Randall Stock helped me design my web site and led me to believe I did it all myself. See for yourself. Here's the domain name: www.trophyenvy.net.

Belanger
Books

Made in the USA
Columbia, SC
28 July 2019